# GET MORE OUT OF YOUR MARCO POLO GUIDE

IT'S

T0166878

**1** go.marco-polo.com/cds

**2** download and discover

# GO!

WORKS OFFLINE!

## SYMBOLS

INSIDER TIP    Insider Tip

★    Highlight

●●●●    Best of…

☼    Scenic view

◎    Responsible travel: fair trade and ecology

(*)    Telephone numbers that are not toll-free

## PRICE CATEGORIES HOTELS

| | |
|---|---|
| *Expensive* | over 150 euros |
| *Moderate* | 90–150 euros |
| *Budget* | under 90 euros |

The prices are for two people sharing a double room in high season without breakfast

## PRICE CATEGORIES RESTAURANTS

| | |
|---|---|
| *Expensive* | over 22 euros |
| *Moderate* | 15–22 euros |
| *Budget* | under 15 euros |

The prices are for a typical dish or daily special, including a drink

On the cover: Museo Picasso in Málaga p. 68 I Flamenco in Granada p. 60

# CONTENTS

---

**DID YOU KNOW?**
Timeline → p. 14
For bookworms & film buffs → p. 23
Local specialities → p. 28
Birdwatching → p. 41
Federico García Lorca → p. 62
The heart of the storm → p. 75
National holidays → p. 113
Spanish addresses → p. 118
Budgeting → p. 119
Weather → p. 121

**MAPS IN THE GUIDEBOOK**
(128 A1) Page numbers and coordinates refer to the road atlas and to the map of Málaga on p. 134/135
(U A1) Refers to the map of Granada inside the back cover
(0) Site/address located off the map.
Plan of the Alhambra on p. 51
Coordinates are also given for places that are not marked on the road atlas

(🛏 A–B 2–3) Refers to the removable pull-out map
(🛏 a–b 2–3) Refers to the additional inset maps of Granada and Málaga on the pull-out map

**INSIDE FRONT COVER:**
The best highlights

**INSIDE BACK COVER:**
Map of Granada

# The best MARCO POLO Insider Tips

## Our top 15 Insider Tips

**INSIDER TIP** **Get a grip!**
Why not take a mountain bike trip, for example, starting in Montecorto in the Sierra de Grazalema run by *Andalusian Cycling Experience*
→ **p. 104**

**INSIDER TIP** **In the footsteps of Russian artists**
The *Colección del Museo Ruso,* an offshoot of the state museum in St Petersburg in Málaga, is a must for art lovers → **p. 67**

**INSIDER TIP** **Heavenly views**
In the Cabo de Gata, take a walk into the mountainous *Vela Blanca*, from where there are magnificent views down onto bays, cliffs and the cape itself → **p. 40**

**INSIDER TIP** **Tapas-hopping in Málaga with insiders**
Tapas bars, small craft shops and food stores: discover with the *Spain Food Sherpas* all those bits of the town you would otherwise miss without them → **p. 70**

**INSIDER TIP** **Poetic pilgrimage**
At the *Huerta de San Vicente* in Granada, you can follow in the footsteps of the great Andalusian poet Federico García Lorca
→ **p. 54**

**INSIDER TIP** **Welcome to the caves**
In the picturesque district of Sacromonte in Granada, you should have a look at the *Cuevas del Sacromonte* ethnographic museum. It comprises eleven cave houses and offers fascinating insights into the cave dwellers' way of life → **p. 57**

**INSIDER TIP** **The real thing**
The stage is set for the emerging talents who perform authentic flamenco at the *Sala Vimaambi,* part of an artists' workshop in Granada → **p. 60**

**INSIDER TIP** **Sci-fi in the desert**
Pay a visit to this futuristic experimental solar energy station, the *Plataforma Solar de Almería* for its powerful message → **p. 38**

# BEST OF...

**FOR FREE**

● *Contemporary art*

CAC is the common abbreviation for the *Centro de Arte Contemporáneo,* the centre for contemporary art based in Málaga. On your visit you will be treated to changing exhibitions showcasing internationally famous artists. What's particularly pleasing is that this experience won't cost you a cent → p. 67

● *Flamenco in Mijas*

You can experience free flamenco every Wednesday at noon on *Plaza Virgen de la Peña* in Mijas, one of the most popular excursions along the Costa del Sol. But only if the weather is fine → p. 86

● *On the trail of historic tomb builders*

Antequera is famous for some very special monuments dating back several thousand years. The *dolmen,* Stone Age burial tombs, are constructed of massive stone slabs balanced on huge side pillars. The town boasts three such dolmen worth mentioning – Menga, Viera and El Romeral – and all three are open to visitors free of charge → p. 71

● *Objets d'art from the Moorish period*

High up on the Alhambra plateau (photo) in Granada the *Museo de la Alhambra* on the lower level of the Palacio de Carlos V presents Hispano-Moorish art from the Middle Ages – interesting displays for free! → p. 55

● *A real highlight for free*

The *Alcazaba* fortress in Almería is a highlight in its own right – and the fact that you can get in without having to pay is the icing on the cake → p. 34

● *Varied summer programme*

In summer, when the little holiday resort Roquetas de Mar puts on its culture and entertainment programme *A Pie de Calle* and the music festival *Pulpop*, it's a real treat, not least for the more money-conscious visitors – all performances are free of charge → p. 37

●●●● Dots in guidebook refer to 'Best of...' tips

### ● *White villages*
Andalusia's white villages are like free open-air museums. Narrow alleyways and staircases wind their way between the bright-white facades; planters and flowerpots provide splashes of colour. *Frigiliana* (photo) in the Nerja hinterland and *Casares* on a ridge in the Sierra Bermeja in the west of the Costa del Sol are particularly beautiful → p. 77, 83

### ● *Gorgeous squares*
Atmospheric squares and promenades are a feature of Andalusia. In essence outdoor living rooms, they are perfect places in which to meet friends. One of the nicest is the *Plaza Bib-Rambla* in Granada, a favourite Old City hotspot → p. 56

### ● *Moorish palaces*
There's nowhere else like it: the *Alhambra* in Granada. Follow the trail of the Moors between the fortifications, the palace complex and the baths. Be seduced by this place of astonishing splendour, with its many pools, amazing stalactite ceiling decorations and forests of columns → p. 50

### ● *Excursion to the 'Snowy Range'*
The *Sierra Nevada,* the 'Snowy Range', rears up within sight of Granada. Mulhacén and Pico de Veleta soar to heights of almost 3500 m/11,500 ft. A mountain road leads up to just beyond the ski resort of Pradollano, but be aware that the snow is only there in winter → p. 63

### ● *Marinas*
Andalusia has a lot of marinas. If you'd like to try one that's a little less busy and at the same time very attractive, make a note of *Marina del Este* at Almuñécar. In contrast, *Puerto Banús* near Marbella is the epitome of expensive chic → p. 48, 90

### ● *Tapas crawl*
No Spanish person would even think of spending a whole evening in a single bar. People typically hop from bar to bar, sampling as many tapas as possible as they go. Why not join them? Granada is a tapas paradise → p. 60

ONLY IN

# BEST OF...

## AND IF IT RAINS?
Activities to brighten your day

● **Science up close**
Particularly for families with kids, there's a whole range of things to see and do at the *Parque de las Ciencias*, from a tropical butterfly park to interactive exhibits and falconry displays. Even worth visiting when the sun's shining! → **p. 109**

● **Crocodile Park**
When it gets a bit cooler outside, the reptilian residents of the *Crocodile Park* in Torremolinos withdraw to the indoor pools – where you can study them up close → **p. 110**

● **Refuge in the Royal Chapel**
The *Capilla Real* in Granada is a cultural-historical gem of the highest order. Due pomp and glory are accorded to Spain's Reconquista royals, who are buried here: Isabella of Castile and Ferdinand of Aragon (photo) → **p. 52**

● **Underwater world**
When it's raining in Roquetas de Mar, escape to a different kind of wet: the town's *Aquarium* awaits you with sharks, rays and all manner of marine creatures → **p. 38**

● **A visit to Picasso**
Housed in a Renaissance palace in Picasso's hometown of Málaga, the *Museo Picasso* is not only for art aficionados. The museum café makes for a great break from the art → **p. 68**

● **Journey under the sea**
When the stormy winds are tearing at the palm trees and the sea is raging beneath a grey sky, your best bet is to take a dive into the underwater world: Málaga's *Museo Alborania* offers visitors guided tours explaining all about what lurks under the waves off the normally sunny coast → **p. 67**

RAIN

# RELAX AND CHILL OUT
## Take it easy and spoil yourself

● *Oasis of peace*

On the patio, on a sun lounger by the pool or in a four-poster bed in one of twelve pleasant, rustically furnished rooms – there are plenty of places to relax at the *Posada Morisca,* a country hotel situated outside Frigiliana → **p. 77**

● *Floating upwards*

Just fifteen minutes to a different world: that's how long the 3-km/1.8-mi ride in the *Teleférico Benalmádena* cable car takes. It will transport you gently from the coastal plain to the summit of Mount Calamorro. On the way you can enjoy some breathtaking views → **p. 87**

● *Bay watch*

Choose a room with a terrace at the *Hotel Doña Pakyta* in the Cabo de Gata Nature Reserve and then just sit back and enjoy the view over the Bay of San José → **p. 43**

● *Fun at the city spa*

Old traditions in new forms: the *Arab Baths* in Granada and Málaga pick up on the customs of the Moorish era. Feel-good oases for relaxing right in the middle of the city → **p. 59, 107**

● *Alhambra view*

The Albaicín district of Granada reveals its unmistakable Moorish origins: narrow alleyways, houses painted a dazzling white. And from the *Mirador de San Nicolás* observation point there is a magnificent view across to the Alhambra. Sit down on the low wall and let your thoughts wander for a while! → **p. 50**

● *On the 'Balcony of Europe'*

In Nerja, if you're in luck and manage to grab a free space on a bench on the so-called 'Balcony of Europe' *(Balcón de Europa),* which is built on a vertical cliff, you can relax and watch all the comings and goings. The wonderful promenade and the viewing platform above the waves is without doubt one of the town's most popular spots (photo) → **p. 74**

INTRODUCTION

# DISCOVER
# THE COSTA DEL SOL!

Up and up it goes: the ride in the cable car from base to summit takes only 15 minutes, but it's a journey into another world, far away from the beaches, the promenades, the high life around the marinas and the resorts with their concrete sprawls. The cable car's shadow glides across the last of Benalmádena's rooftops, over the tops of the pine trees and up the steep slopes. The destination is the 769-m/2523-ft summit of Mount Calamorro, which rises like a throne over the Costa del Sol. Standing in the *soft, gentle breeze*, you gaze down on large parts of the coast laid out before you; far away to the left the suburbs of Málaga reach far inland. Straight ahead on the horizon, boats dot the *gleaming Mediterranean*. And in the distance away to the right – where could that be? A quick rub of the eyes. It might be a little blurred in the haze but there, gingerly revealing itself, is the coast of Morocco.

The proximity of the African continent was a decisive factor in the invasion of Spain in 711 AD that would influence the development of Europe for centuries. Muslim Arabs and Berbers crossed over to the Iberian Peninsula, conquered the kingdom of the Visigoths and remained there for almost 800 years. The Moors called their new lands *Al-Andalus* – the root of the name of Spain's most southerly region of

Check to be sure: 124 intricately carved marble columns grace the Court of the Lions in the Alhambra

Andalusia. They introduced sophisticated irrigation methods in agriculture, built watchtowers and castles and decorated buildings with cool, *colourful tiles*. They also brought with them a new religion, Islam. In the name of Allah they built their mosques and madrassahs and created artisans' quarters, palaces, baths and markets. Spain, particularly the far south, became a melting pot of cultures. Today, the *Moorish legacy* makes a major contribution to the appeal of the Costa del Sol and its hinterland.

In the Middle Ages, the Moors and the indigenous population lived together in reasonable harmony, but this *peaceful coexistence* couldn't last forever. In the north, a resistance began to build, its aim to expel the invaders and eradicate Islam. Reconquista (reconquest) was the term given to this territorial and religious war, which,

**2nd century BC–5th century AD**
Rule of the Romans

**711**
Invasion of the Moors from North Africa across the Straits of Gibraltar; Moorish culture spreads across Andalusia

**8th–11th century**
First cultural and economic flowering of Andalusia under Muslim rule

**13th century**
Start of Nasrid rule in Granada

**1492**
The fall of the Nasrids in Granada marks the completion of the Christian reconquest (Reconquista)

over the centuries, brought the Christians more and more success on the battlefield. The Moorish-dominated area shrank back to the empire of the Nasrid Dynasty of Granada, which extended to the coast of Almería and Málaga. Between the 13th and 15th centuries, there was a last flowering of Moorish high culture. The *Alhambra*, their 'Red Fortress', was conceived as a piece of paradise on earth. In 1492, the glory days were over. Boabdil, the last sultan of Granada, capitulated before the forces of the Catholic Monarchs Isabella of Castile and Ferdinand of Aragon. The fall of Granada meant the end of the Reconquista.

But the region cannot be fully understood without an appreciation of the historic influence and legacy of the Moors. Part of the attraction of Andalusia is its oriental flair. This also radiates from the *white villages*, those peaceful symbols of Andalusia, such as Frigiliana and Casares, which are easily accessible from the coast. With their tight clusters of houses, peaceful corners and steep steps, the villages are a mix of open-air museum and genuine communities. The residents decorate their *labyrinthine alleyways*, entrances and courtyards with *a riot of colourful plants and flowers*. You'll find flowerpots dangling from even the smallest window grill.

> **Floral colour in the courtyards and alleyways**

Culture and villages are one thing, the fascinating landscapes and climate another. With more than *300 days of sun a year*, an eternal spring, Andalusia's 'Sun Coast' lives up to its name and is sometimes dubbed the 'California of Europe'. In summer,

**16th–17th centuries**
Expulsion of Jews and the last Muslims

**1881**
Spain's most renowned artist Pablo Picasso is born in Málaga

**1936–39**
Spanish Civil War followed by dictatorship under General Franco

**1960s**
Economic miracle, onset of package tourism and the first mass development of the Costa del Sol

**1975**
The end of Franco's dictatorship; Juan Carlos I proclaimed king; transition to democracy

15

the resorts heat up in every respect; at other times the region is much more tranquil and mild. The river valleys are sprinkled with *orange groves*, almond trees flourish on the hillsides, and in the desert areas of Almería not much grows at all. Then there are the beaches and volcanic formations of the *Cabo de Gata Nature Reserve*, and the Iberian Peninsula's highest mountains, the Sierra Nevada, with 16 peaks over 3000 m/9800 ft. In the winter, these are covered in snow and ice, and skiers take to the slopes. Scenes and landscapes could hardly vary more – and that also goes for the flora, with gentian and crocuses at higher elevations, pine and oak trees at medium altitudes and the native esparto grass and dwarf palms in the arid lowlands. *Oleander and rockroses* add splashes of colour. Among the flora you might see ibex and golden eagles; a special status falls to the Barbary apes on the rock of Gibraltar – they are the only wild primates in Europe.

Gibraltar marks the westernmost point of the Mediterranean coast of Andalusia. The coast is divided into three large and distinct sections: the Costa del Sol centred on Málaga and Marbella; the *Costa Tropical* focusing on Almuñécar and Salobreña in Granada province; and way over in the east the coast of Almería province. Just as varied as the hinterland are the beaches, whose character ranges from the hidden gems of the Cabo de Gata Nature Reserve to the long golden beaches of Marbella. *Water temperatures* are ideal for bathing from late spring right through to October or November. Rising immediately behind the Costa del Sol and Costa Tropical are mountain ranges such the Sierra de Mijas and the Sierra de Almijara. These block off northerly winds and guarantee a mild climate, in which *avocados and almonds* flourish, along with olives, grapes, lemons and even mangos.

> **Avocados, almonds and olives flourish in the mild climate**

Unfortunately, the original character of some coastal areas is now buried under concrete. Without any foresight and regardless of the consequences for the environment, the construction boom fuelled by mass tourism was set in motion in the 1960s. The tourist industry brought vital foreign exchange to a country, which at that time was one of the poorest in Europe and, until 1975, was under the thumb of the dictator Francisco Franco.

**2008–14**
Real estate and financial crisis weaken Spain

**2009–18**
Exposure of devastating corruption scandals, after which the Spanish prime minister Mariano Rajoy loses a vote of no confidence

**2019**
By tolerating the far-right Vox party, a right-wing coalition under the leadership of the PP replaces the socialist PSOE government

Andalusia's Mediterranean coast has been a favourite among Northern European visitors ever since. Today, the various communities compete with each other for the best *sandy beaches and promenades*; showers and litter-free facilities are now standard. Many beaches have *children's playgrounds*, with slides and climbing frames providing free fun, whether in Marbella or Roquetas de Mar.

Far from the madding crowds: shepherds in the Cabo de Gata Nature Reserve

Many thousands of people, particularly older people or 'part-time' emigrants from Britain, Scandinavia and Germany, turn their backs on Northern Europe and spend a large part of the year soaking up the sun in southern Spain, enjoying breakfast *on the terrace in the middle of winter*. These expatriate residents get together in walking clubs, dance associations, animal welfare societies, charities of various kinds and bridge clubs.

For many locals, tourism is a lucrative source of income, at least in high season, and not just in the restaurants and hotels. Work to live is the motto, rather than the other way around. Even periods of financial crisis cannot dampen the Andalusians' *zest for life* for

## Fiesta and siesta: traditions of Andalusian life

long or destroy their traditions. These include a packed calendar of fiestas and siestas, a first glass of wine around midday, a serious *tapas habit* – and a delight in fun and noise. Get a taste of this love for life, and look forward to a holiday in one of the liveliest, most diverse holiday destinations in Europe.

# WHAT'S HOT

## 1 Eco lifestyle

***Sustainable*** Organic farming is flourishing, thanks to producers such as ◉ *La Molienda Verde (www.molienda.com),* which runs a shop (and restaurant) in Benalauría *(Calle Moraleda 59)* selling jams, pickled chestnuts, etc. Shops such as ◉ *Bio-Natura (Calle Octopus, Bajo 1 | Fuengirola | photo)* also stock organic produce.

## 2 Exquisite titbits

***In the lap of luxury*** The *Mediodía Champagne & Ostras* bar in Marbella's market hall, the *Mercado Central,* entices customers with oysters and 39 (!) perfectly chilled different champagnes. After your Saturday morning shopping spree you can join the locals here in the lap of luxury. The oyster-champagne mix is available in Málaga too: at the champagne bar *La Medusa (Calle Santa María).*

## 3 Daytime revellers

***Beach clubs*** Beach clubs don't only party after darkness falls! At *Purobeach Marbella (Ctra. de Cádiz km 159 | Laguna Village | Playa El Padrón | Estepona | www.purobeach.com | photo)* you can relax by day to some chill-out rhythms, before things really start hotting up in the evening. At the *Ocean Club Marbella (Av. Lola Flores | Nueva Andalucía | www.oceanclub.es)* dancers and DJs will brighten up your day, and there are concerts at *Sala Beach (Urbanización Villa Marina | Puerto Banús | www.salabeach.com).*

# Fabulous fashion

*Fashion* The Costa del Sol is colourful and vibrant – and this is especially reflected in its fashion. Pepa Karnero's *Pepaloves* range is sweet and streetwise at the same time. For her urban-look prints, this *Malagueña* designer is inspired, among other things, by the creativity of regional street artists. Here on the Costa del Sol you'll find her clothes in Estepona at *Vai Vai (Av. de España 124)*, at *Bámbola (Av. de Andalucía 108)* in Caleta de Vélez and in Granada at *Cuca (Av. Dilar 12). Find de Luxe Vintage (Calle de Casapalma 9 | Málaga | photo)* really lives up to its name; the shop sells unique second-hand items which share the rails with redesigned pieces from the 1960s to the 1990s. Quality fashion with a story, both exclusive and original – unique textile art.

## Alternative lifestyle

*Alternative* Costa del Sol is not just a long string of fashionable and modern coastal resorts. In the hinterland especially, time seems to have stood still – firmly anchored in some cases in the 1960s and 1970s. You can discover this side of the region at the *Artisans' Market (every first and third Sunday in the month)* in Órgiva. After an approximately 40-km/24-mi drive north of Marbella you arrive at the *Molino del Rey (Alozaina | www.molinodelrey.com)* in the Valle de Jorox, a small, exclusive yoga resort with accommodation for just 20 guests. It offers spa and beauty treatments and various weekly courses, focusing on holistic wellbeing: topics range from meditation and mindfulness, Hatha and Vinyasa yoga down to the role of proper nutrition.

# IN A NUTSHELL

## ALMERÍA – THE MOVIE MECCA

In the 1960s, filmmakers hit upon the idea of making the province of Almería the location for Westerns and shifted their sets from Arizona, Texas and New Mexico to the scorching sun of Southern Spain. In the desert and steppe-like areas around Tabernas and the Cabo de Gata, they made their movies about cowboys and Indians, outlaws, adventurers and Mexican revolutionaries. Nowadays film fans can track down former celluloid backdrops through Western villages and along designated 'cinema routes'. Compared with the gold-digging atmosphere of the past, things have calmed down a little in the film province of Almería. But the golden colours of the dry region still managed to attract the location scouts for Ridley Scott's Bible adaptation 'Exodus: Gods and Kings', while the mighty walls of Alcazaba of Almería were recently transformed into one of the capital cities in the 'Game of Thrones'.

## BULLFIGHTING

Man against beast, but the winner is certain because the meat has already been sold before the unequal contest begins. When it comes to bullfighting, the *corrida de toros*, opinions are divided. Traditionally minded Andalusians get drunk on the drama, the magnificence of the toreros, and the bravery and strength of the bulls. For its supporters, the *aficionados,* the bullfight is considered an art. For most non-Spanish people – and in-

**From immigration to environmental protection: notes about the passion for flamenco, the culture of the Moors and the daily ritual of siesta**

creasing numbers of Spaniards as well – the ritual is nothing more than a brutal massacre that should be abolished. Among politicians this concern falls on deaf ears, such is the power of the bullfighting lobby and the amount of money flowing into this sector of the economy.

But the belief continues to grow, even among its proponents, that bullfighting, whose current rules were devised in Ronda in Andalusia, must change. *Tauromaquia*, which includes not only the *corrida* but also all the cultural trappings, has been proposed for cultural heritage status. For that to happen, the spectacle will have to become more politically correct. On Majorca and the other Balearic Islands, for example, bloody bullfighting has been prohibited by law since 2017, meaning the animals can neither be injured nor killed by the toreros. But such a solution seems very far off in Southern Spain.

## CAVE DWELLINGS

In Granada's district of Sacromonte and in the little town of Guadix, the landscape is riddled with caves where people have lived for hundreds of years. The caves are actually man-made, and it all began in the late Middle Ages when people in Guadix needed storage and places of refuge. Over time, whole districts of cave dwellings emerged; today, this may seem like an archaic way to live, but the caves are well appointed, just like any other Spanish home, and without the musty smells you might expect. Between the whitewashed walls there is a constant temperature of

# CRISIS PHENOMENA

In better days the Costa del Sol was one of the biggest beneficiaries of the building boom, when one new housing estate sprang up after another. When the real estate bubble burst in 2008, the whole of Spain's economy began to reel and many construction projects were stopped. Even though real estate prices on the Mediterranean coast are slowly recovering, evictions, so-called *desahucios*, continue to be part of everyday

In and around Guadix: the extraordinary cave and grotto dwellings

18°–20°C (64°–68°F). Modern amenities have long since arrived, in the form of electricity, running water, TV and Internet. In Guadix and Granada, cave museums provide a fascinating look at life in these dwellings, whose occupants include many *gitanos* ('gypsies'). In Sacromonte, some caves have been turned into venues for flamenco shows; in Guadix you can even stay in cave hotels.

life. Numerous signs saying 'Se Vende' (for sale) or 'Se alquila' (for rent) testify to the huge number of empty properties. Despite new laws that strengthen tenant rights and give the state the right of first refusal in order to prevent forced sales, there were more than 10,000 cases of foreclosure in Andalusia in 2018 alone. The result is social exclusion, often leading to children having to move back home to their parents, with up to three generations living under one roof.

# ENVIRONMENTAL PROTECTION

Officially about one fifth of the area of Andalusia is protected in one way or another, but environmental awareness is not always followed through. On the one hand, schoolchildren go out and plant trees and there are commendable individual initiatives to clear rubbish; on the other, economic interests and corruption often seem to take the upper hand. Apartment and hotel projects go ahead despite the fact they contravene Spain's own laws concerning coastal development.

There are a large number of exclusive golf courses, which require huge quantities of precious water. In arid areas, the traditional wells dried up long ago due to overuse, and the precious supplies have to be extracted from ever-greater depths. The same principle applies to the irrigation of the swathes of greenhouses in Almeria province, which cover tens of thousands of hectares around El Ejido. Beneath shiny plastic sheeting, vegetables ripen for export in double quick time: cucumbers, peppers, aubergines, courgettes, and various types of salad; or tomatoes that are perfectly round and red but contain little in the way of flavour, just lots of pesticides to maximise profits. The prognosis for the future of this exploited landscape is very gloomy. Some scientists believe, however, that climate change is not only a threat to the region but can also be an opportunity – to deal more responsibly with soils, water and natural resources.

# FLAMENCO

Staccato heels, a pounding rhythm. Love, that deepest of emotions, always lies at the heart of flamenco. There are different ways to express it: in song *(cante)*, instrumental performance *(toque)* and dance *(baile)*. The history of flamenco is inextricably linked to the *gitanos*, or 'gypsies' Excluded from mainstream

# FOR BOOKWORMS & FILM BUFFS

**As I Walked Out One Midsummer Morning** – Laurie Lee's beautifully evocative tale (1969) about his travels through Spain in the 1930s, including some fascinating descriptions of the towns and villages of the Costa del Sol, which have since changed so radically

**A Fistful of Dollars** – Classic 'Spaghetti Western' directed by Sergio Leone (1964), who mostly used the desert scenery of Almería province as the location. A young Clint Eastwood is in top form with his revolver

**The Lemons Trilogy** – Three entertaining books by Chris Stewart, co-founder of the rock band Genesis and now an author and farmer living in the Alpujarra

**The Disappearance of García Lorca** – Movie thriller from 1996 (also available on DVD) about the dangerous search for what exactly happened to the poet Federico García Lorca, who was murdered outside Granada just before the outbreak of the Civil War. Starring Andy Garcia and Esai Morales

Despite the lobby, the *corridas* no longer go unchallenged even in Andalusia

society since time immemorial, the *gitanos* sought solace and togetherness through their songs. The Romani, who originally came from India, settled in Andalusia in the 15th century and currently make up 3.6 per cent of the population. Suffice to say that in the course of the 19th century flamenco became socially acceptable, although it was often distorted by the clichéd image of vivacious gypsy women. Flamenco has long been recognised as an art form, split into several dozen genres, and is continually evolving. Although the 'gypsies' are often regarded with suspicion and still live on the margins of society, flamenco gives them dignity and respect. Flamenco schools have come into fashion. Outsiders can get a first taste of the art of flamenco by seeing a show at one of the hole-in-the-wall cave venues in the Sacromonte district

of Granada, though commercialisation does tend to compromise authenticity. In 2010, flamenco was inscribed by Unesco on the representative list of intangible cultural heritage of humanity.

# MMIGRATION

While Andalusia has attracted Eastern Europeans (who in some cases have left the region again because of the economic crisis) in search of work and thousands of Northern Europeans, who enjoy the good life in the sunshine, there is no end to the press reports about illegal immigration from Africa. In mostly unseaworthy boats called *pateras,* exhausted boat people wash up again and again on the shores of Andalusia. All they carry with them is the hope of a better life, but Spain, wracked by its own economic crisis, has worries of its own. If they don't end up being repatriated, the immigrants find seasonal work as farm labourers on starvation wages, or in more fortunate cases as kitchen or home helps or in the building trade. Others end up as hawkers – you see them travelling around selling counterfeit CDs and clothes.

# NDIGNADOS

When protesters began setting up camp on the Plaza del Sol in Madrid on 15 May 2011 protesting at high unemployment, corruption and social injustice, the wave of discontent also swept as far as the Costa del Sol. Spin-off groups of the *Movimiento 15-M* or the *Indignados* ('The Outraged') were founded in many places. In 2014, politics professor Pablo Iglesias set up the left-wing party *Podemos,* and local groups such as the *Costa del Sol Sí Puede* formed on the Costa del Sol. All have the same goal: to put an end to corruption and cronyism in politics and offer a new perspective for young people in particular. But even the party, which was long seen as the hope of the left, has since struggled to adjust to everyday politics and is in danger of breaking up into several camps and regional groupings. In Andalusia around 41 per cent of 25-year-olds have no job and only one in three have sufficient financial resources to be able to leave home and live independently. This lack of prospects has led many young people to go abroad. In relation to the population, the number of emigrants leaving the provinces of Málaga and Granada were the greatest in the country in 2018: of every 1000 inhabitants, an average of 8 to 9 set off in search of happiness abroad.

# MOORS

In 711 AD, the Moors came across the Straits of Gibraltar from North Africa and initiated a cultural golden age in Andalusia. In the 11th century, power struggles in their own ranks resulted in the flourishing Caliphate of Córdoba disintegrating into small kingdoms (taifas), while Christian troops from the north began advancing on their campaign of reconquest, the Reconquista. The last Muslim powerbase was that of the Nasrid Dynasty in Granada, which survived until 1492, when the Catholic Monarchs Ferdinand of Aragon and Isabella of Castile triumphed over the enemies of the faith. With this final victory over the Moors, the royal couple secured the territorial integrity of Spain and laid the foundations for the country's rise to the status of a great European power. A major part of Andalusia's touristic appeal comes down to what the Moors left behind, and you'll encounter their medieval legacy almost everywhere you go in Andalusia – in the architecture, the magnificent gardens with their ingenious irrigation systems and fountains, in the cuisine, as well in many place names, words and geographical areas, including all those starting with 'al' or 'guadal'.

# SIESTA

It is a daily ritual and an integral part of the southern lifestyle: the siesta, or midday break. The length of the siesta is flexible, and depends on how long lunch takes. But it happens sometime between 3 and 4.30 or 5pm. Even if the mandatory lunch break is ever more contentious, especially among Spanish employees, life in Southern Spain almost grinds to a halt at this time of day, with many businesses, monuments and museums closing. The reason for having a siesta is simply the hot southern climate. How are you supposed to work with the sun beating down from the sky? A short nap enables people to recharge the batteries for the second half of the day, which is shunted into the cooler hours of the evening. Why don't you give this routine a try!

Magnificent legacy of the Moorish era: water gardens such as at the Alhambra

# FOOD & DRINK

Andalusians really like their food. Large chunks of their budget and their time are spent savouring culinary delights. If you consider yourself a connoisseur of beautifully prepared food, go to a tapas bar and sample a wide range of little treats.

Tapas are *appetisers*. Although they are now widely eaten just about everywhere outside Spain, they hardly ever taste as good as they do here, in their place of origin. It is impossible to define what makes a good tapa – there is an almost endless variety, ranging from *fried calamari* to artichokes with anchovies or slices of air-dried ham on bread. The bars of Granada enjoy a special status – as a general rule you'll automatically get tapas served with your wine or beer – tasty little morsels at no additional cost (though in reality they are covered by the cost of the drinks).

No local would ever think of spending the whole time in one bar. In the evening in particular, the convention is to hop from one bar to another in search of the most original and delicious tapas. On the other hand, it is not common to go Dutch: if you're in a group, the best way to *pay is with a joint kitty* or to take it in turns to pay for everything. And by the way, INSIDER TIP the sign of a good bar is a messy floor, covered in used napkins, toothpicks and olive stones, left there by appreciative locals. Clearly, hoards of locals have just left, so it must be good, and it's worth trying a mouthful even if it's *dreadfully overcrowded*.

Photo: gazpacho

**The key here is to change bars frequently –
it's the only way to sample as many
Andalusian tapas as possible**

Dipping in and out of tapas bars is part of the daily routine in Andalusia. It is a part of a custom that might initially seem alien to many Northern Europeans – as might the landlady of a small country inn cheerfully announcing that breakfast will be served between 9 and 11am! It is generally a good idea to try adapting to the rhythm of Andalusia, where everything *shifts forward a couple of hours*.

Lunch isn't served until 1.30 or 2pm, and dinner doesn't happen before 9 or 10pm. In tourist areas, restaurants are more likely geared to earlier meal times (or even serve throughout the day); hardly an authentic, Spanish practice. Nor is levying a cover charge *(cubierto*; beware, this is a rip-off) or putting English food on the menu or serving a full English breakfast!

The Spanish like their **breakfasts** sweet rather than salty, and in small quantities. A croissant or toast with jam, accompanied by a milky coffee *(café con leche)*, an espresso *(café solo)* or an espresso with a shot of milk *(cortado)* usually suffices.

# LOCAL SPECIALITIES

**aceitunas** – olives; good with wine or a freshly pulled beer *(caña)*

**ajo blanco** – a cold soup made with garlic, almonds and grapes

**boquerones** – anchovies either deep-fried *(fritos)* or marinated in vinegar, olive oil and garlic *(en vinagre)*

**chorizo** – spicy pork sausage with garlic and paprika; can be eaten raw, cooked in a stew or fried with a splash of sherry or red wine

**chuletillas de cordero lechal** – suckling-lamb chops

**churros con chocolate** – deep-fried dough rings dunked in thick drinking chocolate; especially good in the morning after a night on the town (photo left)

**gambas al ajillo** – prawns fried with garlic and olive oil (photo right)

**gazpacho** – cold soup with tomatoes, peppers, cucumber, onions, garlic, vinegar, olive oil and white bread

**jamón de Trevélez** – air-dried Serrano ham from the mountain village of Trevélez in the Alpujarra

**pescaíto frito** – small fish, deep-fried in a coating of batter; *the* speciality in beach restaurants and bars

**pincho moruno** – skewers of marinated meat

**plancha, a la** – prepared on a glowing hotplate – fish and meat as well as vegetables

**plato alpujarreño** – hearty dish from the Alpujarra: a platter with black pudding *(morcilla)*, pork sausage *(longaniza)*, air-dried ham, fried egg, sauté potatoes and occasionally a piece of pork loin *(lomo)*

**rabo de toro (estofado)** – (stewed) oxtail

Tea drinkers will be disappointed with the rather bland-tasting teabag in hot water; however, sipping a *fresh mint tea* in a Moorish inspired teashop *(tetería)* in Granada is a different proposition altogether. A light breakfast like this means that by 11am or noon you'll be looking forward to *aperitifs* and the first tapas of the day before lunch.

The *daily specials menu (menú del día)* is always a good choice, but if a three-course meal is too heavy for you in the middle of the day, there is usually the option of something lighter, such as a mixed salad *(ensalada mixta)*, a baguette sandwich *(bocadillo)* or a few tapas. Similarly, a ham or cheese platter can be ordered as a whole portion *(ración)* or **half portion** *(media ración)*; **seafood** also comes as a *ración*.

In tourist centres, you'll also find paella on menus, even though it's originally a Valencian dish. In a good paella you should be able to recognise and taste the individual ingredients – from vegetables (including peppers and tomatoes) to seafood (including mussels and squid) and meat (pork, chicken and rabbit), depending upon the type of paella you order.

**Fish dishes** are popular but don't come cheap. Rising expenses and over-fished oceans play a role here, although salmon, for example, comes almost exclusively from farms. Favourite fish and seafood dishes include sea bass *(lubina)*, monkfish *(rape)*, octopus *(pulpo)* and small squid *(chipirones)*.

In the evenings, top restaurants cater to discerning guests with taster menus. Such a menu, which can easily cost 50 euros or more, enables the chef to show off what he/she can do. However, even though the Spaniards in the south of the country love their food, they tend to prefer what is known as the **dieta mediterránea**: the use of healthy and balanced ingredients – lots of vegetables, fruit, garlic, olive oil and fish.

**Quality wines** can be distinguished by the protected designation of origin *(Denominación de Origen)* on the label. Alongside red wine *(tinto)*, rosé *(rosado)* and white wine *(blanco)* there is also dessert wine made of muscatel grapes (e.g. *vino de Málaga*). For beer drinkers, good Spanish brews include San Miguel and Mahou. If you want a **draught beer** order a *caña*; a *cerveza* normally comes bottled, often in small sizes (0.25 l or 0.33 l); a further variation is alcohol-free beer *(cerveza sin alcohol)*. Because of the high level of chlorine in tap water, it's better to order mineral water *(agua mineral)*.

It isn't just the strong dessert wines that are typical of Andalusia, but also **sherry**,

A drop of *fino* is the ideal tapas accompaniment

produced in the area around Jerez de la Frontera. One shouldn't order a 'sherry' but state specifically the required type – *fino* for a dry sherry, *amontillado* for a medium and *oloroso* for a sweet sherry.

# SHOPPING

Artisan traditions and the large number of visitors make this part of Andalusia a shopper's paradise. In Granada's atmospheric Alcaicería, which was once the Moors' silk bazaar, visitors will think they've been carried off to the Orient. However, there is quite a lot of overpriced and stereotypical rubbish: castanets and flamenco costumes made of cheap material, and tourist tat made in China.

In contrast, authentic art and crafts reflect the influences of the various different cultures that have left their mark on the region: Phoenicians, Iberians, Romans and especially the Moors. The youthful Spanish fashion scene from Madrid and Barcelona has also spread to Andalusia. While places like Puerto Banús concentrate on smart boutiques, in Almería and Granada things are a bit more down-to-earth. Leather shoes are generally cheaper than they are at home. *Fluchos* is a top-quality brand – handsewn shoes for men and women.

## CULINARY ITEMS

Jars of marinated olives *(aceitunas)* are inexpensive and easy to transport, as are tins of liver pâté made from the flavoursome black Iberian pork *(paté de higado de cerdo ibérico)*. If you can, make use of the service and have a spicy *chorizo* or a nice piece of Serrano ham shrinkwrapped *(envasar al vacío)* for the journey home.

However, should you be tempted to buy a complete leg of ham, perhaps in the Alpujarra town of Trevélez, you should be aware that without the aid of a ham stand *(jamonero)*, holding and cutting the joint will be a struggle!

A sweet speciality is the **INSIDER TIP** traditional sugarcane syrup *(miel de caña)* from Frigiliana. If you're here with your own car, it's worth leaving room for a couple of bottles: extra virgin olive oil *(aceite de oliva virgen extra)*, wine, grape marc brandy *(orujo)* from the Alpujarra or dessert wine from Cómpeta.

## INLAY WORK

*Taracea* is the name given to the Moorish-inspired inlay work that you'll see on jewellery boxes, chessboards, mirror frames, trays, musical boxes and tables. The craftsmen create beautiful mosaics

**There are real treasure troves for souvenir hunters – but the boundary between art and kitsch is often blurred**

from a variety of materials, including bone fragments, mother-of-pearl and precious woods.

## MARKETS

Street markets *(mercadillos)* take place at fixed times and places. The colourful stands and stalls that are set up in coastal towns such as Nerja, Fuengirola, Torremolinos, Estepona and Marbella are particularly popular.

## MUSICAL INSTRUMENTS

Not only will you hear the sound of flamenco on every street corner in Granada, the city is also a stronghold of guitar builders. Today there are still more than two dozen guitar workshops in the province of Granada. They make both classical and flamenco guitars.

## POTTERY

Look out for glazed plates, bowls and mugs with green and blue designs on a white background. This classic look dates back to the time of the Nasrids, the last Moorish dynasty in Spain. Pots, cups and saucers are also available. There is a particularly wide choice in Granada.

## RAG RUGS

*Jarapas* is the name for the INSIDER TIP rag rugs, that are sold in the larger mountain villages of the Alpujarra. This traditional craft, whereby strips of waste cloth are woven into colourful rugs, has given rise to a thriving cottage industry. At once attractive and reasonably priced souvenirs, small rag rugs cost from around 7–8 euros, larger ones around 25–30 euros. You will also find bags, blankets and curtains made of the same material.

# ALMERÍA & COSTA DE ALMERÍA

Interested in Wild West sets and mirages? Rocky landscapes in shades of brown and ochre, rugged mountains dropping to the sea, sheltering glorious little beaches? Do you like the idea of remote bays without any kind of development – not even a shack? Then, in the Cabo de Gato Nature Reserve, you're in just the right place.

This is the driest region in all Spain. The light is blinding, the sea crystal clear. Dried-out riverbeds furrow the landscape, the rocky slopes are fissured and cracked. Once a poor, forgotten part of the world, nowadays the Costa de Almería is being discovered by those with a taste for adventure. Here you will find the most unspoilt and deserted beaches in the whole of Southern Spain. Deserted

also means there is little in the way of infrastructure. A good base is the coastal town and port of San José, the starting point for hikes, mountain bike tours and dusty tracks leading to beautiful beaches. In complete contrast to this wild scenery is the area around El Ejido, the centre of extensive plastic greenhouse cultivation, and the built-up parts of the coast around Aguadulce and Roquetas de Mar. The largest city is Almería, the provincial capital, where the last remnants of those arid mountains disappear into the sea.

## ALMERÍA

(133 D5) (*M5*) Al-Mariyya, 'Mirror of the Sea', is the name the Moors gave to

Photo: Playa del Mónsul at Cabo de Gata

Semi-desert, arid mountains, summer heat: the sun-baked province of Almería is like an outpost of Africa in Europe

**CITY WHERE TO START?**
Obviously it has to be the omnipresent **Alcazaba!** It's best reached on foot or on the L1 bus. Buses and trains arrive at the Estación Intermodal (Plaza de la Estación); from there it's about 1 km/0.6 mi to the edge of the centre. There are conveniently located car parks on Plaza López Falcón, Plaza de San Pedro and Avenida Federico García Lorca.

**the capital (pop. 196,000) of the province of Almería.**

Almería is a lively harbour town, and though it cannot compare with Granada or Málaga in terms of flair and attractions, it is also less crowded with tourists. The cultural highlight of the provincial capital is the Moorish fortress Alcazaba, which towers over the old town. Caliph Abd al-Rahman III gave the order for the construction of the huge defensive complex in the middle of the 10th century. The fort offered space for

The climb up to the Alcazaba takes your breath away – but then so does the view from the top

20,000 soldiers and allowed for perfect control over the harbour, around which the town's economy still resolves. The 16th-century cathedral forms the focal point of the old town.

## SIGHTSEEING

### ALCAZABA ★ ● ☀

The entrance to the 10th-century Moorish citadel leads up a zig-zag ramp and through the horseshoe Gate of Justice, the *Puerta de la Justicia,* beyond which is an expansive area of ramparts, towers and terraced gardens. Historians estimate that the gigantic complex could house up to 20,000 people. Between the citadel and sea stand old town houses, roof terraces and the port with its cold stores and loading cranes. In the gardens of the castle precinct, cypresses and palm trees cast their shadows, and fountains and water channels deliver their coolness to peaceful corners. Hedges and flowerbeds

are beautifully tended. A second wall protected the central fortress, but little remains of that now. The Christian conquerors constructed their own castle at the highest point of the Alcazaba at the beginning of the 16th century – a symbol of the triumph over Islam crowned by the Tower of Homage, the *Torre del Homenaje. April–mid-June Tue–Sat 9am–9pm, mid-June–mid-Sept 9am–3pm and 7pm–10pm, mid-Sept–March 9am–6pm, Sun all year round 9am–3pm / entrance free for EU-citizens, otherwise 1.50 euros | entrance via Calle Almanzor*

### OLD TOWN

You will sometimes feel like you are in a small village in the tranquil alleyways of the old town. Behind the bulky cathedral there is lots to learn about Spanish guitar building at the interactive *Museo de la Guitarra (Tue–Sun 10.30am–1.30pm, Fri/Sat also 5pm/6pm–8pm/9pm | 3 euros | Ronda del Beato Diego Ventaja s/n |*

loading facility at the harbour near the Avenida Federico García Lorca. The *Monument to Tolerance*, right next to the Cable Inglés, has commemorated the Spanish victims of the Nazi concentration camp Mauthausen since 1999. 142 cement columns represent the 142 Almerienses who died as forced labourers in the camp.

### CATHEDRAL

After the recapture of Almería from the Moors in 1489, another menace soon appeared from across the sea – Barbary corsairs. With the constant fear of attack from these pirates, the cathedral was built as a fortified structure, battlemented and with hardly any windows – it looks more like a castle than a church. Work on the cathedral continued into the 18th century and consequently produced a mix of Gothic, Renaissance and Baroque styles. The defensive character of the building continues in the elongated interior, where the lights on the walls resemble torches. At the east end, how-

*almeriacultura.es | approx. 45 min).* A couple of blocks further towards the harbour, take a look inside the *Centro Andaluz de Fotografia (daily 11am–2pm, 5.30pm–9.30pm | entrance free | Pintor Diaz Molina 9 | www.centroandaluzdelafotografia.es).* North of the cathedral on Plaza de la Constitución is the 1899 town hall and the modern *Centro de Interpretación Patrimonial*, which vividly tells the story of the city's history using interactive elements (also in English). *(Tue–Sun 10.30am–1.30pm, Fri/Sat also 5pm/6pm–8pm/9pm | entrance free | Plaza Vieja | www.almeriacultura.com).* It is not far to the small Plaza Flores, on which a John Lennon in bronze strums away on a guitar.

### CABLE INGLÉS & MONUMENTO A LA TOLERANCIA

A must for nostalgic architecture fans, this giant iron construction from the beginning of the 20th century is a historic ore

★ **Alcazaba in Almería**
Between battlements, towers and garden terraces – under the spell of this 1,000-year-old castle → p. 34

★ **Desierto de Tabernas**
Dramatic landscapes straight out of a Western – the desert of Tabernas → p. 37

★ **Cabo de Gata Nature Reserve**
One of the last coastal paradises in southwest Europe → p. 39

★ **Cala de la Media Luna**
'Half Moon Bay' is a dream of a beach → p. 42

**MARCO POLO HIGHLIGHTS**

ever, the ambulatory behind the altar has exquisite star vaulting. *Daily, opening times vary, see website | 5 euros incl. audio guide, entrance free | Plaza de la Catedral | catedralalmeria.com*

## FOOD & DRINK

### CLUB DE MAR ☆☆

Behind the marina, steps lead up to this spacious restaurant, which has windows looking out over the harbour. The culinary emphasis is on fish and seafood. *Closed Tue | Playa de las Almadrabillas 1 | tel. 950235048 | rcmalmeria.com | Moderate–Expensive*

### TAPAS

*Taberna La Encina (closed Sun evening and Mon | Calle Marín 16 | tel. 950273429 | restaurantelaencina.net), Taberna Nuest-ra Tierra (Mon only mornings | Calle Jovellanos 16 | tel. 679897432 | taberna nuestratierra.com)* and Casa Puga *(closed Sun | Calle Jovellanos 7 | tel. 950231530 | barcasapuga.es)* are popular tapas bars. In places like these, it is customary in Almería to serve free tapas with beer and wine. They're not really 'free', though, as the drinks cost a bit more than usual. The combined price, drink plus tapa, is around 2.20–2.60 euros.

## BEACHES

The beaches start in the southeastern part of town, with the popular *Playa del Zapillo-El Palmeral.* Walkers, joggers, cyclists and skaters are out and about along the palm-lined promenade of the *Parque de Nicolás Salmerón* until late in the evening.

All good gifts come from above: *Ibérico* ham in Casa Puga

## ENTERTAINMENT

The 'Game of Thrones' film crew were spotted drinking at the popular *Pub Burana (daily | Paseo de Almería 56)*. There is occasionally live music at *La Cueva (daily | Calle Canónigo Molina Alonso 23 | www.lacueva-almeria.com)*. The flamenco bar *Peña El Taranto (Tenor Iribarne s/n | www.eltaranto.com)* uses the Moorish *Aljibes árabes de Jairán* cistern as an atmospheric backdrop.

## WHERE TO STAY

### HOTEL CATEDRAL ALMERÍA

Four-star comfort and elegance on Cathedral Square, in a building dating from the mid-19th century. There are four different room types and price categories. The stylish *Restaurante La Catedral* is located inside. *20 rooms | Plaza de la Catedral 8 | tel. 9 50 27 81 78 | www.hotelcatedral.net | Budget–Moderate*

### TORRELUZ CENTRO

Right in the centre of town, offering good value for money. With satellite TV and its own garage. The *Nuevo Torreluz* on the same square is more expensive and rates two more stars. *24 rooms | Plaza de las Flores 8 | tel. 9 50 28 14 29 | www. torreluz.com | Budget*

## INFORMATION

*Parque Nicolás Salmerón, corner of Calle Martínez Campos | tel. 9 50 17 52 20 | www.turismodealmeria.org* (city), *www. turismoalmeria.com* (province)

## WHERE TO GO

### AGUADULCE (133 D5) (*M5*)

The rather unattractive new apartment complexes in the coastal town of Agua-dulce (pop. 14,000) are in stark contrast to one of the most attractive marinas in Andalusia *(puertodeportivoaguadulce.es)*. Situated just beyond the end of a nice beach, the marina is the hub of the local nightlife scene, with music bars and restaurants.

### DESIERTO DE TABERNAS ★
(133 D–E 4–5) (*M4*)

The ground is dusty and stony, baked dry and dissected by cracks and fissures.

Under the steely-blue sky the scenery is dominated by dramatic rock formations, with colours ranging from dark browns to rusty reds. Leave the A92 to Granada at the Tabernas exit, approx. 20 km/13 mi north of Almería, and follow the N340 for a spot of desert sightseeing from the comfort of your own car. The road leads through a genuine desert *(desierto)*, and if you think the scenery looks like it's straight out of a Western movie, you'd be spot on. Classics such as 'The Magnificent Seven' and Sergio Leone's 'Once Upon a Time in the West' were filmed here. Almería became an important movie location, and the legacy remains at the old Western film sets along the route: *Oasys* (see the 'Travel with Kids' chapter) and the *Cinema Studios Fort Bravo – Texas Hollywood (in summer daily 9am–8pm, western shows usually at 12.30 and 7pm, otherwise daily 9am–6pm with shows at 12.30, 2.30pm and 5.30pm | www. fortbravooficial.com)*. Tepees, a palisade fort and a dusty settlement stand out from the landscape; the gallows, sheriff's office, church and saloon create the Wild West atmosphere. The authentic set is well worth visiting for Western fans, although it is quite pricey. *Tabernas* itself, which lies a little further along the main road towards Murcia, is dominated by its 11th–12th-century Moorish castle, but there's not much else to see.

**INSIDER TIP** **PLATAFORMA SOLAR DE ALMERÍA** ⊕ (133 D–E4) *(⊞ M4)*

The solar energy research facility in the desert of Tabernas exploits the climate. More than 3200 hours of sunshine per year are an inexhaustible resource for the production of solar energy at one of the world's most important research centres of its kind. Visiting the complex, which is situated some 30 km/19 mi north of Almería, is like being transported onto the set of a science fiction movie. It is surrounded by the desert mountains, and you'll find yourself among endless rows of panels, shiny pipe systems, turbines and the solar power station with its 80-m-/260-ft-high tower. Established at the beginning of the 1980s, the work of the complex is based on difficult processes and a very simple concept – to find the cheapest and most environmentally friendly ways of utilising energy from the sun. The visitor centre offers guided tours. *Mon–Fri 8.30am–4.30pm (compulsory registration). Entrance depends on group size | Ctra. de Senés km 4.5 | tel. 9 50 38 79 90 | psa.es*

## ROQUETAS DE MAR (133 D6) *(⊞ M5)*

Just like the neighbouring town of Aquadulce, the sprawling resort town of Roquetas de Mar (pop. 80,000), just 20 km/ 13 mi southwest of Almería, is principally a package tourism destination now dominated by hotels and apartment blocks. More appealing than the building developments are the attractive promenades, beaches with showers, groups of palm trees and children's playgrounds. And *Playa de la Romanilla* is absolutely immaculate. The restored *Castle (Tue–Sat 10am/ 11am–1pm, 5/6pm–8/9pm, Sun 10am–1pm, guided tours Tue–Fri 11am and noon | entrance free)*, dating from the 16th century, draws many visitors and now hosts temporary exhibitions. Concerts are held in the modern *Teatro-Auditorio*. Families with children will want to head for the ● *Aquarium (June–Sept daily 10am–9pm, Oct–May Mon–Fri 10am–6pm, Sat/Sun 10am–7pm | entrance 16.95 euros, children (aged 3–14) 12.95 euros | Av. Reino de España s/n | www.aquarium roquetas.com)*, where sharks and rays ply the waters, or the neighbouring *Mario Park* (see 'Travel with Kids' chapter). *www.roquetas-de-mar.es*

3200 hours a year: the sun heats up the mirrors at the Plataforma Solar

# CABO DE GATA NATURE RESERVE

**(133 E–F 5–6)** *(🗺 N5)* ⭐ **There is nowhere else in Spain with such a variety of geographical features! Volcanic rock formations, salt flats, mountains as dry as a bone, and hidden bays are all to be found along the 60 km/37 mi of mostly unspoilt coastline that constitutes the** *Parque Natural Cabo de Gata-Níjar.*

Spread across the almost 200-square-mile reserve, a quarter of which is a marine reserve, are villages, farms and a network of minor roads. You need to have your own car to explore. The best base is San José, though it's important to note that much of the accommodation closes down during the winter. Officially, the reserve is called Cabo de Gata-Níjar, but the community name of Níjar is usually left off because its main centre lies outside the reserve boundary. In the south, the Cabo de Gata, a rugged headland, juts out into the sea. Geologically the region was formed during several volcanic phases that occurred between 6 and 15 million years ago. Ash cones, lava flows and the typical cone-shaped hills such as the Morrón de los Genoveses above the bay of the same name are a legacy of this bygone era of volcanism.

Even though greenhouses and vegetable plantations come right up to the edge of the reserve, a series of fortunate circumstances has protected the coastal strip from greater inundation from agriculture and tourism. Intriguingly, pirates can be regarded as the founding fathers of the reserve. The constant threat from the sea saw to it that the coast remained largely free of settlements, other than some minor defences constructed during the 18th century. The barren mountains and hills,

The little resort of La Isleta del Moro lies on the neck of a peninsula

which reach all the way to the beaches, have a steppe and semi-desert character. Half an hour of rain in November is treated as a major event here; between April and October there is normally no rain at all. Only the nightly mist delivers enough moisture to enable small bushes of herbs, esparto grass and dwarf palms to survive.

## PLACES IN THE NATURE RESERVE

**CABO DE GATA** ☼ **(133 E6)** *(∅ N5)*
Vertical cliffs, a lighthouse and churning seas – Cabo de Gata has all the classic features of a cape, but even more spectacular and magical is the neighbouring formation of *Arrecife de las Sirenas,* the 'Mermaid's Reef', whose rocks rise out of the sea like needles. This is a mini maritime mountain range, the remnants of a volcanic chimney. Until the mid-20th century it was home to colonies of monk seals, the origin of the 'mermaids' in the name. According to superstition among

local fishermen, the sounds they heard were not produced by these animals at all, but by mermaids. The only road to the cape leads from the little village of *San Miguel de Cabo de Gata* (often just called El Cabo de Gata), where there is a small promenade and old watchtower in the sand, down the flat western section of the reserve via La Almadraba de Monteleva. Either side of San Miguel a pebbly beach stretches away for around a mile. Evidence that salt is still being extracted from the local flats is provided by the mounds near the side of the road just before La Almadraba.

A detour from the cape into the rocky promontory ☼ **INSIDER TIP** *Vela Blanca* provides the best views in the reserve. Whether you're here by car or on foot, you get there as follows: some 300 m before the car park at the cape, take the inconspicuous little road to the left past dwarf palms and the car park above the bay of Cala Rajá. Beyond this, the road – which is in pretty poor shape – winds its way into the hills for 1.6 km/1 mi, where the historic watchtower of Vela Blanca and a modern radio transmitter act as beacons. The road ends at the transmitter – with wonderful views of the cape. At your feet, below the nearby watchtower, is the east coast of the reserve, studded with bays, leading towards San José. The track going down to beaches and bays such as Cala de la Media Luna is closed to traffic but not to mountain-bikers or hikers. Because of the wide inland loop motorists still have another 30 km/19 mi from the Cape to San José.

### LA ISLETA DEL MORO 🌟
**(133 E5–6) (*⌂ N5*)**
The little resort and fishing village not far from Pozo de los Frailes sits on the neck of a headland jutting into the sea. There is a beautiful view across the bay to the Frailes Massif.

### RODALQUILAR (133 E5) (*⌂ N5*)
The eerie shells of abandoned buildings and deserted ponds at the edge of this village recall the days when there was a gold rush in these parts. Gold was discovered here in 1883, and hundreds of workers were employed in the mines right up until the 1950s. But by 1966 all the seams had been worked out. 'Minas de

Oro' signs in the centre of the village direct you to the concrete ruins. On the approach to the village, beautiful views of the coast open up from the 🌟 *Mirador Las Amatistas* viewpoint.

The Nature Reserve Visitor Centre, the *Centro de Visitantes Las Amoladeras (tel. 9 50 16 04 35 | www.parquenatural.com),* lies a few miles northeast of San Miguel near Ruescas/Rambla de Morales; the route there is clearly signposted.

# SAN JOSÉ

**(133 E6) (*⌂ N5*) Several small hotels and restaurants make San José (pop. 2000) the largest and most convenient base for exploring the Cabo de Gata Nature Reserve.**

San José is situated on a broad bay on the east coast of the nature reserve. Its brilliant white houses stretch just a short distance inland, for the bay is dominated by the rugged foothills of the Sierra de Cabo de Gata including the 500-m-/1640-ft-high Frailes Massif. It is a cul-de-sac at the southern end of the only access road

# BIRDWATCHING

Some 500–600 pink flamingos live in the salt flats of the Cabo de Gata Nature Reserve all year round. In summer, their numbers rise to up to 2500. It's possible to get a good view of the birds from freely accessible hides: just before San Miguel de Cabo de Gata to the left of the road (coming from the direction of Rambla de Morales) or,

even better, from the Observatorio Las Salinas on the stretch between San Miguel and the cape (signposted to the left). With a bit of luck, you should also be able to spot grey and silver herons, black-winged stilts, cormorants and avocets. It's possible to do an approx. 11-km (7-mi) hike around the salt flats.

from inland (via El Pozo de los Frailes). After that, a single track leads southwest to beautiful beaches such as Los Genoveses and Media Luna. This track is accessible by car (if you're hiring a car check in advance the terms and conditions in the hire agreement to ensure you can go off road) as well as mountain bike. In San José itself, life revolves around the Plaza de Génova, with its palm trees, the Paseo Marítimo beach promenade and motorboat and yacht marina.

## FOOD & DRINK

### EL JARDÍN

Here on the sports harbour the pizza is baked using organic ingredients and tastes delicious. There are many vegetarian and vegan options on the menu alongside fish and meat. Dishes can also be prepared gluten or lactose free on request. *Closed Tue–Wed | Calle Puerto Deportivo, Local 8 | tel. 6 21 21 40 42 | restauranteeljardin.com | Budget–Moderate*

### CASA PEPE

This traditional bar with a dreamy terrace right over the bay specialises in healthy slow food and the furnishings are fittingly minimal. *Daily | Calle Correos 79 | tel. 9 50 38 08 57 | casapeperestaurante.es | Moderate*

## BEACHES

From the southwest end of San José a track runs parallel to the coast for approx. 8 km/5 mi; along the way are turnoffs to the beach car parks. Occasionally a bus service runs from San José in summer; schedules vary from year to year and are therefore unpredictable. Outside the peak summer months, you'll have long stretches of beach almost all to yourself.

The *Playa de los Genoveses* curves like a sickle towards the volcanic cone of Morrón de los Genoveses; in the central section of the beach there are fossilised dunes. Between the beaches of Genoveses and Mónsul lies *Playa Barronal,* an official nudist beach. You can get there if you leave your car at the track car park and then trudge across the dunes for about 10 minutes. More easily reached are the last beaches off the track: *Playa del Mónsul* and Cala de la Media Luna, both with dusty car parks behind them. Enclosed at each end by rocky headlands, the 300-m-/990-ft-long 'Half Moon Bay' ⭐ *Cala de la Media Luna*, with its fine sand and crystal-clear water, is everything that an unspoilt, heavenly little beach should be – except for the fact that there is no shade whatsoever. Along the coast in the direction of the cape, the eye wanders along the craggy mountainside, the colours alternate between ochre, chalk white and rusty brown, and the Vela Blanca promontory rises up in the background.

If you want to explore the reserve north of San José, the nicest beach is *Playa de los Muertos* between Agua Amarga and Carboneras.

## RECREATION & TOURS

From San José, the travel agency *Grupo J 126 – Rutas de la Naturaleza (Av. de San José 27 | tel. 9 50 38 02 99 | www.cabodegata-nijar.com)* organises **INSIDER TIP** jeep tours and walks. A night-time walk in summer will take you beneath the starlit skies of the semi-desert. For the daytime tours, don't forget water and sun protection! Another agency, *Medialunaventura (Calle del Puerto 7 | tel. 9 50 38 04 62 | www.medialunaventura.com),* offers 2- to 3-hour **INSIDER TIP** sea kayak tours.

The bizarre coastline of the Cabo de Gata Nature Reserve is volcanic in origin

For a great unguided mountain bike tour through the reserve, follow the dirt track southwards from San José (bike hire available) down to the beaches. Beyond the last one, Cala de la Media Luna, pass the barrier and ascend the track as it makes a broad loop into Vela Blanca hills, up towards the old watchtower and radio transmitter. Then descend to the cape along a pot-holed tarmac road. Return the same way: total distance approx. 25 km/16 mi. It's tough going, so sun protection and plenty of drinking water are absolutely essential!

Follow the track from San José for a short distance towards Playa de los Genoveses, and at the hill beneath the windmill take the signed footpath *Sendero Los Genoveses*, diagonally to the left. The target from here is the *Morrón de los Genoveses*, a volcanic cone above the beach around 2 km/1.2 mi away.

Beyond Playa de los Genoveses experienced hikers INSIDER TIP can follow the coast from bay to bay as far as Playa del Mónsul. Caution: the route doesn't follow the water's edge but goes slightly inland, passing along sometimes very steep scree slopes and through very deep depressions. The path is not always recognisable.

## WHERE TO STAY

### INSIDER TIP HOTEL DOÑA PAKYTA
● ☀

A stylish little hotel, where the higher price for the terrace with its beautiful panoramic view of the bay is well worth it. Steps lead from the hotel directly to the beach. Restaurant on terrace in summer. *13 rooms | Calle Correo 51 | tel. 9 50 61 11 75 | www.playasycortijos.com | Moderate*

### EL DORADO

A friendly *hostal* on an elevated position in the centre. The rooms are nicely kept. *27 rooms | Camino de Aguamarina | tel. 9 50 38 01 18 | www.hostaleldorado.com | Budget*

### SANTUARIO SAN JOSÉ

Simple *hostal* with own restaurant, within easy walking distance of beach and harbour. *28 rooms | Calle de Cala Higuera 9 | tel. 9 50 38 05 03 | www.elsantuario sanjose.es | Budget*

# GRANADA & COSTA TROPICAL

Between the rugged coast and the high ridges of the Sierra Nevada at 3481 m/11,421 ft this region has enormous geographical and scenic variety. And from a cultural and historical perspective the city of Granada, with its labyrinthine Albaicín quarter and stunning Alhambra, takes you on the trail of the Moors. The oriental magic exuded by the Alhambra, with its riot of arches, arabesques and stalactite decoration, is unmatched in Europe.

On the coast, the region is not particularly known for picture-perfect beaches; all along the Costa Tropical, however, there are hidden bays such as Cantarrijan (nudist, stony) and Marina del Este (small, pebbly). A good springboard for some of the lesser known beaches is the little town of Almuñécar. Here, the beaches are mostly stony gravel, but the water is exceptionally clear.

People here don't live from tourism alone. There are plantations of orange trees, almonds, olives and **INSIDER TIP** chirimoyas, or custard apples, as these potato-sized, calcium-rich fruits of the Costa Tropical are also known. Underneath the green skin with its characteristic honeycomb pattern lurks a white, creamy, slightly sour-tasting flesh with lots of seeds. You are well advised to tackle these with a spoon!

The other great culinary indulgence of the region is its wide range of tapas. Leisurely explorations of the city's pubs and taverns are an integral part of a visit to Granada.

The highest mountains on the Spanish mainland, a 'tropical coast', and at the heart of it all the bustling city of Granada with the amazing Alhambra

# ALMUÑÉCAR

**(131 E5) (∅ J5) Fresh air, 320 days of sunshine annually and broad beach promenades are among the attractions of this hub of the Costa Tropical.**

The gravel beaches hug a series of spits and promontories, interrupted by the cliffs of Peñón del Santo. The coastline is completely built up, a fate that Almuñécar shares with the holiday resorts of Costa del Sol to the west.

For all the modern development, the little town (pop. 26,000) looks back on a long and eventful history, starting with the Phoenicians, who established a settlement here around 2800 years ago. The remains of their fish-curing plant *(fábrica de salazones)*, which was later taken over by the Romans, lie in the Park El Majuelo, below the castle. The oldest part of town, with its twisting alleyways and whitewashed houses, is in the Upper Town, between the castle and the Archaeological Museum. Here, potted plants flank the doorways, and

Seen from up on the Peñón del Santo Almuñécar's beaches lie at your feet

strangers still receive a friendly welcome from the older residents of the town. This is in stark contrast to the hustle and bustle of the Calle Real area near the town hall. The mountain barrier of the Sierra de Almijara rises up behind the town.

## SIGHTSEEING

### CASTILLO DE SAN MIGUEL AND MUSEO ARQUEOLÓGICO CUEVA DE LOS SIETE PALACIOS ⚠

A stone bridge spans the moat and leads to this interesting, labyrinthine fortress. Even though the ground plan is from the Moorish period, the round towers were first added in the 16th century. The climbs and descents between the old and newly restored masonry are fantastic for playing at knights. The entrance ticket will also get you into the *Archaeological Museum (Calle San Joaquín s/n)* in the cave complex of Cueva de los Siete Palacios, which was inhabited back in the Bronze Age and was used as a Minerva temple by the Romans. *Nov–March Tue–Sat 10.30am– 1.30pm and 4pm–6.30pm, Sun 10am–*

*1pm, April–Oct Tue–Sat 10.30am–1.30pm and 5/6.30pm–7.30/9pm, Sun 10.30am– 2pm | entrance 2.35 euros | Explanada del Castillo s/n*

### PARQUE ORNITOLÓGICO LORO SEXI

Information on Almuñécar's Bird Park in the 'Travel with Kids' chapter.

### PEÑÓN DEL SANTO ★

The rock separates the two main beaches in Almuñécar. Seventy-five steps take you up to the tiled ⚠ esplanade. Take your time to let your gaze wander and enjoy the view over the sea and the bare mountain ranges dotted with white houses in the hinterland.

## FOOD & DRINK

Tapas, tapas, tapas – that's the order of the day around *Plaza de la Constitución (Town Hall Square)*, *Plaza Kelibia* and behind *Paseo Puerta del Mar*, but it's hard to say which restaurant is the best. Fish and shellfish are the order of the day at the beach restaurant *Calabre* on Playa de San Cristóbal. *Summer daily, otherwise daily except Tue | Paseo de las Flores 2 | tel. 9 58 63 00 80 | Moderate*

## BEACHES

The beaches extend from *Playa Velilla* in the east, via *Puerta del Mar* and *Caletilla,* which are close to the town, to the long *Playa de San Cristóbal* in the west, where fishing boats often lie pulled up on the beach.

## SPORTS & ACTIVITIES

Scream down the slides at the saltwater park *Aqua Tropic* (153 E5) on Playa de Velilla *(mid-June–start of Sept daily 11am–7pm | entrance 23, children (aged 12–15) 17, (aged 4–11) 15 euros, cheaper online | Paseo Marítimo | www.aquatropic.com).*

On guided plantation tours, e.g. at *Finca San Ramón (La Herradura, N–340 km 309.1 | fincasanramon.net)* you will find out more about the cultivation of exotic fruits such as mangos, lychees and papayas on the Costa Tropical.

## WHERE TO STAY

**HELIOS COSTA TROPICAL**
Its convenient location near the beach of San Cristóbal is just one advantage of this hotel block. Many ⚓ rooms with sea view; the hotel also has a pool. *227 rooms | Paseo de las Flores 12 | tel. 9 58 63 06 36 | www.hoteleshelios.com | Moderate*

## INFORMATION

*Palacete de la Najarra | Av. de Europa 12 | tel. 9 58 63 11 25 | www.turismoalmune car.es, www.almunecar.info*

## WHERE TO GO

**LA HERRADURA (131 E5) (∭ H5)**
*Herradura* means 'horseshoe', derived from the horseshoe-shaped bay on

---

★ **Peñón del Santo in Almuñécar**
A rocky promontory with a view along the coast of Almuñécar → p. 46

★ **Albaicín in Granada**
Out and about in Granada's most atmospheric district, with wonderful views of the Alhambra → p. 49

★ **Alhambra in Granada**
Its palaces and courtyards make this 'Red Fortress' one of the wonders of the world → p. 50

★ **Capilla Real in Granada**
The funerary chapel of the Catholic Monarchs, with its magnificent marble tomb → p. 52

★ **Tapas bars in Granada**
There's a great atmosphere in the university city's bars with their delicious appetisers → p. 60

★ **Salobreña**
The most beautiful white village along the Costa Tropical → p. 48

★ **Barrio de Cuevas in Guadix**
Unique in Spain: thousands of people live in underground caves to this day → p. 62

★ **Sierra Nevada**
The highest mountains on the Iberian Peninsula have skiing in the wintertime → p. 63

**MARCO POLO HIGHLIGHTS**

which this town of 4000 inhabitants is situated. Everything happens along the 2-km-/1.2-mi-long coarse-grained beach, which is bound by a lively promenade. The water sports on offer, e.g. windsurfing at *La Herradura (windsurflaherradura. com)*, are just as good as the culinary options: *Chiringuito El Bambú (daily | Paseo Andrés Segovia | tel. 9 58 82 72 27 | www.chiringuitoelbambu.com | Moderate)*. In the colourful open-air *La Cochera (daily | Paseo Andrés Segovia 45 | tel. 6 92 03 78 23 | facebook: La Cochera La Herradura | Budget–Moderate)* you'll almost feel like you're in Goa. La Herradura doesn't have the atmosphere and character of your typical 'multinational' tourist resort; it tends to be mostly Spanish families who come here.

### MARINA DEL ESTE ●
### (131 E5) (*ØD H–J5*)
One of the prettiest marinas in Andalusia, located approx. 5 km/3 mi southwest of Almuñécar. Enclosed by steep hills and rocky promontories that drop abruptly into the sea, it is a peaceful little place, with a couple of outdoor restaurants in which to while away a pleasant lunchtime. Nearby is the *Playa Marina del Este,* a 150-m pebble beach.

### INSIDER TIP ▶ PLAYA DE
### CANTARRIJÁN 〰 (131 D–E5) (*ØD H5*)
This official nudist beach *(playa naturista),* approx. 12 km/7.5 mi west of Almuñécar, is stony and extends for about 300 m between two rocky headlands. A beach restaurant usually opens in the high season, otherwise visitors enjoy the seclusion and the scenic beauty of the cliffs, which are part of a small nature reserve, the *Paraje Natural Acantilados de Maro-Cerro Gordo.* The beach can be reached down a short, 1.4-km/1-mi road that turns off the 〰 N340 in

the direction of Nerja. It runs high above the coast and is well known for its fantastic views. The beach is also nice for non-nudists!

### SALOBREÑA ★ (131 E5) (*ØD J5*)
A dramatic crag topped by a castle and white sugar-cube houses tumbling down the hillside, Salobreña rises from the coastal plain, 15 km/9 mi east of Almuñécar. Steep alleyways lead to the upper village where the 〰 *Paseo de las Flores* promenade surrounds the castle hill – the view of the Sierra Nevada is stunning. Good, authentic fare is to be had at 〰 *Restaurante Pesetas (closed Mon | Calle Bóveda 11 | tel. 9 58 610182 | www.restaurante-pesetas.es | Budget–Moderate)* as well as at the beach restaurant *El Peñón (daily | Paseo Marítimo s/n | tel. 9 58 61 05 38 | www.restaurante elpenon.es | Budget–Moderate).*

# GRANADA

### ░░ MAP INSIDE THE BACK COVER
### (131 E3) (*ØD J4*) **Granada, shortened to Graná in the Andalusian dialect, is one of the most beautiful cities in Spain. It is a place that lives and breathes history at every turn; a city of students, plazas, promenades, bars and intimate corners.**
Lying at the foot of the Sierra Nevada at a height of around 700 m/2300 ft, the provincial capital (pop. 240,000) occupies a broad plateau, the Vega de Granada. In the 13th century the Nasrid Dynasty made Granada the heart of their empire, a piece of the orient in the occident, the last bastion of the Moors on the Iberian Peninsula. The Catholic monarchs Ferdinand and Isabella regained the city during the Reconquista in 1492; Sultan Boabdil surrendered his Alhambra, the 'Red Fortress', without a struggle.

A Moorish fortress dominates the old heart of Salobreña, seaside resort for the Granadans

Drivers should give the city a wide berth. In parts of the city, there's a video-monitored ban on private vehicles, something that isn't always obvious to outsiders. There's also a shortage of car parks, and many of the hotels don't have their own garage. The car park on *Plaza de San Agustín (empark.com)* is centrally located, but not very cheap. Or follow the parking guidance system. The car park at the Alhambra is reached by following the well-signposted approach loop. A good alternative to expensive multi-storey car parks is to park just outside the city and take a taxi into the centre. Once there, it's easy to get around on foot or by bus (overview of routes on *www.transportesrober.com*). If the climb up to the Albaicín or Sacromonte proves too tiring, simply hop aboard one of the public minibuses (routes C31, C32, C34). To reach the Alhambra, walk up from Plaza Nueva via the Cuesta de Gomérez or take bus routes C30 and C32. The new metro line connects the bus station well out of town on Carretera de Jaén with the slightly more central RENFE train station, but doesn't go into the city centre. Bus no. 33 will take you from the bus station right into the city.

## SIGHTSEEING

### ALBAICÍN ★ (U D–E2) (*M d–e2*)

Narrow alleyways criss-crossing the hillside; whitewashed houses with roof terraces and tiny patios; cypress trees, palm trees, potted plants, bougainvilleas, overhead wires, colourful tiles on the walls and the occasional patch of peeling paint or plaster: that is the Albaicín

> **CITY** **WHERE TO START?**
> The best place to soak up the atmosphere of the city is around **Plaza Bib-Rambla (U C4)** (*M c4*). You can then saunter through the bustling Alcaicería; from there it's not far to the Cathedral and the Royal Chapel.

Up and down the steps of the Albaicín through alleyways decorated with tiles and flowers

(also spelled Albayzín) quarter, once home to a substantial Muslim population. On the pedestrian street of *Calderería Nueva,* shady teashops *(teterías)* help to recreate the Moorish atmosphere. The quarter's alleyways climb steeply, culminating at the ● ☆ *Mirador de San Nicolás,* with magnificent views of the Alhambra. Nearby, the mosque ☆ *Mezquita Mayor (www.mezquitade granada.com)* INSIDER TIP (accessible garden and viewpoint) reflects the fact that Muslims were not banished forever in 1492 – in fact, several thousand Muslims still call Granada their home. There is another viewpoint, the ☆ *Mirador de San Cristóbal,* on the northernmost edge of the Albaicín, near the main road to Murcia.

## ALHAMBRA ★ ●
(U D–E 3–4) (ᗰ d–e 3–4)
Imposing from the outside, paradise on earth inside, the Alhambra was based on an ingenious concept. Constructed between the 13th and 14th centuries for the rulers of the Nasrid dynasty, the cen-

tral palace precinct was surrounded by massive, crenellated walls for protection and camouflage. This precinct, the *Palacios Nazaríes,* forms the heart the Alhambra, which is ranged across a plateau high above the ravine of the Darro River. Ornate strapwork, intricately carved stucco, horseshoe arches, forests of columns, arabesques and calligraphy (pictorial representations are forbidden by Islam), stucco ceiling decorations and repeated rhombus patterns are just some of the typical Moorish features you will encounter during a tour of the Palacios Nazaríes. The entrance to the precinct leads through the former courtroom, the *Mexuar,* which was converted into a chapel by Catholic monarchs, to the first richly decorated courtyard, the *Patio del Cuarto Dorado.* From here, a passageway leads through to the Court of the Myrtles, the *Patio de los Arrayanes,* where myrtle hedges frame a long pond in which the walls of the adjacent Torre de Comares are calmly reflected, creating one of the Alhambra's most enchanting vistas. The tower houses the Ambassadors' Hall, the *Salón de Embajadores,* where the Nasrid rulers received foreign diplomats. Spanned by a canopy consisting of 8017 individual pieces of cedar wood, it is the largest hall in the Alhambra.

A passage leads from the Court of Myrtles to the exquisite Court of the Lions, the *Patio de los Leones,* the basin of its central fountain supported by 12 marble lions. The filigree arcade surrounding the patio incorporates 124 marble columns. This courtyard provides access

to the *Sala de los Abencerrujes* and the *Sala de las Dos Hermanas,* both of which have ceilings of the most amazing stalactite stuccowork. It was also the way to the harem. All the rooms were heated by charcoal braziers, while the mashrabiyyah shutters enabled people to see out without being seen themselves.

Pools and gardens are integral to the palace complex, and beautiful views open out over the Albaicín. Apart from the Palacios Nazaríes there are three further

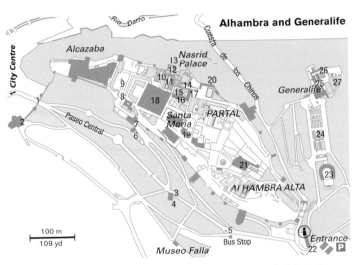

**Alhambra and Generalife**

1 Puerta de las Granadas
  (Pomegranate Gate)
2 Torres Bermejas
  (Red Towers)
3 Fuente del Tomate
  (Tomato Fountain)
4 Monumento a Ganivet
  (monument to writer
  from Granada)
5 Fuente del Pimiento
  (Paprika Fountain)
6 Pilar de Carlos V
  (Column of Charles V)
7 Puerta de la Justicia
  (Gate of Justice)
8 Puerto del Vino
  (Wine Gate)

9 Plaza de los Aljibes
  (Cistern Court)
10 Mexuar (former audience
  chamber)
11 Patio de los Arrayanes
  (Myrtle Court)
12 Salón de Embajadores
  (Ambassadors´ Hall)
13 Torre de Comares
14 Sala de las Dos Hermanas
  (Hall of Two Sisters)
15 Patio de los Leones
  (Lion Court)
16 Sala de los Abencerrajes
  (Hall of the Abencerrajes)
17 Sala de los Reyes
  (Hall of the Kings)

18 Palacio de Carlos V
  (Palace of Charles V)
19 Baños (baths)
20 Torre de las Damas
21 Parador de San Francisco
22 Entrance to Alhambra
  and Generalife
23 Theatre
24 Jardines nuevos
  (New Gardens)
25 Patio de la Acequia
  (Pool Court)
26 Patio de la Sultana
  (Court of the Sultana)
27 Jardines altos
  (Upper Gardens)

areas in the Alhambra: on intricate paths and wide promenades, past parks, fountains and carefully pruned hedges, the way leads up to *Generalife*, the Nasrids' summer palace with its famous water features in the *Patio de la Acequia*. In the bailey of Alcazaba, where the guards' houses, silos and stables were once located, the tower of *Torre de la Vela* is worth climbing for the wonderful panorama of the city and the mountains.

Parts of the Alhambra had to make way for the building of the *Palacio de Carlos V* as well as the neighbouring *Santa María church* in the 16th century. The monumental Renaissance palace, quadratic on the outside, round on the inside, served as a symbol of the triumph over Islam. Through the cool, colonnaded palace court you reach ● *Museo de la Alhambra (Wed–Sat 8.30am–6pm, mid-March–mid-Oct until 8pm, Mai–Sept Sat until 9.30pm, Tue, Sun always 8.30am–2.30pm | entrance free | www.alhambra-patronato.es)* with Hispano-Moorish art from the Middle Ages. On the upper floor the museum presents the fine arts *(Museo de Bellas Artes | Tue–Sat mid-Oct–March 9am–6pm, April–mid-Oct 9am–8pm, Sun all year round 9am–3pm | entrance free for EU citizens, otherwise 1.50 euros | www.museosdeandalucia.es/web/museodebellasartesdegranada)*. It includes historical views of the Alhambra as well as works by the Granada painters Alonso Cano (1601–1667) and Manuel Gómez Moreno (1870–1970).

The perfect place for refreshment is the neighbouring *Parador* in the former Franciscan convent: you'll find cool tranquillity with a magical Alhambra panorama on the café terrace of the classy hotel. A visit to the Alhambra needs planning in advance. As the tickets are often sold out weeks in advance, make sure you reserve yours in good time at *www.alhambra-tickets.es or tel. 8 58 95 36 16*. A maximum of 10 tickets per person can be booked. You will need a credit card and the names and passport numbers of every visitor for the booking. You can print out the tickets yourself or pick them up from the counter or the ticket machines at the entrance. You can buy same day tickets directly from the Alhambra ticket office if the allocation is not depleted. Entry into the Palacios Nazeríes is only possible at the printed time, without exception. *April–mid-Oct daily 8.30am–8pm, late evening visit Tue–Sat 10pm–11.30pm, mid-Oct–March daily 8.30am–6pm, late evening visit Fri/Sat 8pm–9.30pm, late evening visit Generalife only April–mid-Nov | entrance for whole complex 14, without Palacios Nazaries 7, late evening visit Palacios Nazaríes 8, late evening visit Generalife and gardens 5 euros | www.alhambra-patronato.es*

The *Granada Card (entrance to the main sights and 9 trips on public transport / 40 euros, valid for 5 consecutive days / www.granadatur.com/granada-card)* has its own allocation of Alhambra tickets, so it's certainly worth buying.

### EL BAÑUELO *(U D3) (⟮ d3)*

An inconspicuous entrance leads to the 11th-century Arab baths. In medieval times Granada had 21 of these thermal baths, and for the Moors they weren't just for washing but also for resting the mind and body as well as socialising. A small courtyard provides access to the former sauna and relaxation rooms with their well-preserved brick walls and vaults, horseshoe arches and star-shaped skylights. *Tue–Sat 10am–2pm | Carrera del Darro 31*

### CAPILLA REAL ★ ● *(U C3) (⟮ c3)*

The late Gothic splendour of the Royal Chapel attached to the Cathedral is the

This cool, green idyll is an oasis of calm: the Moorish gardens of the Generalife

setting for the tomb of Spain's most important royals: Isabella of Castille (1451–1504) and Ferdinand of Aragón (1452–1516), the 'Catholic Monarchs'. Under their rule, during which Moorish Granada fell and Columbus discovered America, a new era was ushered in for the whole of Europe. The Italian Domenico Fancelli created the tomb, which is adorned with marble effigies of the royal couple. The chapel is also the last resting place of the heir to the Castilian throne, Joanna the Mad (1479–1555) and her husband Philip the Handsome (1478–1506), as well as one of Ferdinand and Isabella's grandchildren. Steps lead down into the simple crypt containing the five lead coffins. The showpieces in the adjacent museum are Ferdinand's sword and Isabella's crown and sceptre. *Spring/summer Mon–Sat 10.15am–1.30pm and 4pm–7.30pm, Sun 11am–1.30pm and 2.30pm–6.30pm,* *autumn/winter Mon–Sat 10.15am–1.30pm and 3.30pm–6.30pm, Sun 11am–1.30pm and 2.30pm–5.30pm | Calle Oficios 3 | www.capillarealgranada.com*

### CARMEN DE LOS MÁRTIRES
(U E5) (*ℳ e5*)

This garden ensemble on the Paseo de los Mártires is ideal for a short break. Peacocks scream and water splashes in the ornamental fountains surrounding the white 19th-century palace. *Mid-March–mid-Oct Mon–Fri 10am–2pm and 6pm–8pm, Sat/Sun 10am–8pm, mid-Oct–mid-March Mon–Fri 10am–2pm and 4pm–6pm, Sat/Sun 10am–6pm*

### CASA DE LOS PISA (U D3) (*ℳ d3*)

The Casa de los Pisa is an especially beautiful and well-preserved Renaissance palace, notable for its **INSIDER TIP** fine courtyard. The palace contains a museum dedicated to the memory of San Juan de Dios (1495–1550). The saint spent the last part of his life in Granada, where he devoted himself to serving the

The guided tour takes about 30 minutes and leads into the lounge, kitchen and the piano room, which is graced by a painting by Lorca's friend, Salvador Dalí.

The overwhelming dimensions of Granada's cathedral: a gigantic declaration of faith

poor and needy, founding a charity hospital and caring for the sick and the lame. *Mon–Sat 10am–2pm | Calle Convalecencia 1 | www.museosanjuandedios.es*

**INSIDER TIP CASA-MUSEO FEDERICO GARCÍA LORCA (HUERTA DE SAN VICENTE)** (U A5) (*ⅅ a5*)

Once well outside the city, this former estate is now on its outskirts and within earshot of the traffic on the ring road. The chalk-white property served as the summer home of Federico García Lorca and his family from 1926 to 1936; here Andalusia's greatest dramatist found the time and space to create new works.

Upstairs, Federico's room contains his bed and desk, other rooms are used for temporary exhibitions dedicated to the poet's life and work. The Huerta de San Vicente is surrounded by the beautifully laid out Parque García Lorca. On Wednesdays admission to the museum is free! *Tue–Sun 9.15am–2.15pm, April–mid-June and 2nd half of Sept also 5pm–8pm, Oct–March also 4pm–7pm | Calle Virgen Blanca | www.huertadesanvicente.com*

**INSIDER TIP CASA-MUSEO MANUEL DE FALLA** (U E4) (*ⅅ e4*)

Manuel de Falla (1876–1946) is one of Spain's greatest composers. Between

1922 and 1939, the year he migrated to Argentina, he lived in this *carmen,* a typical Granada-style whitewashed villa with blue shutters. Here, high above the rooftops of the city, he enjoyed 'the most beautiful view on earth', as he described it. He entertained many famous artist friends in the salon. The painter Ignacio Zuloaga liked to come here, as did Federico García Lorca and the later Nobel prize-winning poet Juan Ramón Jiménez. A guided tour of the house takes in the kitchen, the composer's studio with its piano, and the bedrooms of Falla and his sister. A lot of Falla's belongings have been preserved, including his collection of ties and hats. *July/Aug Wed–Sun 9am–2pm, Sept–June Tue–Fri 9am–2.30pm and 3.30pm–7pm, Sat/Sun 10am–2.30pm | Calle Antequeruela Alta 11 | www.museomanueldefalla.com*

### CATHEDRAL (U C3) (*⋒ c3*)

More than 100 m long, Granada's cathedral is known for its vast proportions. First begun in 1518 by Enrique Egas, then continued from about 1530 in Renaissance style by Diego de Siloé, its construction carried on until 1704. Alonso Cano's Baroque facade was one of the last elements to be incorporated, but even then the tower remained incomplete. Inside the cavernous interior it is easy to feel lost amid the enormous columns, organ pipes and Cano's huge canvases. Alonso Cano (1601–1667) was a painter and sculptor as well as an architect *(Mon–Sat 10am–6.30pm, Sun 3pm–5.45pm | entrance 5 euros incl. audio guide, Sun free entrance when reserving at archidiocesis granada.es | catedraldegranada.com*

### CENTRO FEDERICO GARCÍA LORCA (U B–C3) (*⋒ b–c3*)

The centre houses the Lorca Foundation archive and serves to conserve and maintain the work of the Andalusian poet and dramatist. *Tue–Sat 11am–2pm and 6pm–9pm (winter 5pm–8pm), Sun 11am–2pm | Plaza de la Romanilla | www.centrofederi cogarcialorca.es*

### CORRAL DEL CARBÓN (U C4) (*⋒ c4*)

This 14th-century Moorish building, once a coal merchants' inn, is now home to an open-air cultural centre with a programme of concerts, theatre, dance courses and the legendary Los Veranos del Corral flamenco festival in summer. The city's best singers, guitarists and dancers take to the stage. *Calle Mariana Pineda*

### MONASTERIO DE LA CARTUJA (O) (*⋒ O*)

Founded in 1506, this Carthusian monastery is situated a little outside central

# LOW BUDGET

You can buy the *Granada Card* city ticket online at *www.granadatur.com* and in Granada's municipal tourist office on Plaza del Carmen. There's a choice of two types ('Basic', valid for 3 days, and 'Plus' for 5 days) costing 33.50 and 37.50 euros respectively. Both include admission to the Alhambra and cathedral as well as 5 (or 9) free rides on public buses.

Admission to the lower level of *Palacio de Carlos V* in Granada is free. It houses the ● *Museo de la Alhambra (Tue and Sun 8.30am–2.30pm, Wed–Sat 8.30am–6pm, mid-March–mid-Oct until 8pm)* with its displays of Hispano-Moorish art from the Middle Ages such as ceramics, stucco and inlay work.

Granada, but it is well worth a visit for the exuberant Baroque decoration of the church and sacristy. *April–Oct, daily 10am–1pm and 4pm–8pm, Nov–March 10am–1pm and 3pm–6pm | Paseo de la Cartuja*

## MONASTERIO DE SAN JERÓNIMO
(U B2–3) *(*📍 *b2–3)*

After the fall of Muslim Granada, and with the support of the Christian monarchy, it didn't take long for various religious orders to establish themselves in the city. They included the Hieronymites, who were responsible for this monastic complex built in 1504–1563. Today it is home to a tiny community of the female branch of the order. Highlights of a visit are the two-storey cloisters with orange trees and a nice view of the bell tower, and the vaulted interior where the main chapel has a magnificent altarpiece with INSIDER TIP colourful and ornate reliefs and sculptures. *April–Oct daily 10am–1.30pm and 4pm–7.30pm, Nov –March 10am–1.30pm and 3pm–6.30pm | Calle Compás de San Jerónimo 9*

## MUSEO CAJA GRANADA (O) *(*📍 *O)*

First off, the most important part of this multi-functional block is the fine-art department which includes works by Pablo Picasso, José Guerrero and Santiago Rusiñol, among others. It is also the venue for INSIDER TIP cultural events such as theatre, cinema and concerts. *Sept–June Tue–Sat 9.30am–2pm, Thu–Sat also 4pm–7pm, Sun 11am–3pm, July Mon–Sat 9am–3pm, Sun 11am–3pm | Av. de la Ciencia 2 | www.memoriadeandalucia.com*

## PALACIO DE CARLOS V (U E3) *(*📍 *e3)*

With its square ground plan enclosing an open, round courtyard with a diameter of around 30 m/100 ft, this palace is an unusual structure. Only two of the three storeys that were originally planned were actually completed. Today the lower level houses the *Alhambra Museum* (see also p. 55); above it is the *Museum of Fine Art (Museo de Bellas Artes | mid-June–mid-Sept Tue–Sat 9am–3.30pm, mid-March–mid-June and mid-Sept–mid-Oct 9am–8.30pm, mid-Oct–mid-March 9am–6pm, Sun all year round 9am–3.30pm | www.museosdeandalucia.es).* Among the highlights of the collection are the historic depictions of the Alhambra as well as works by local-born artists Alonso Cano (1601–1667) and Manuel Gómez Moreno (1870–1970). The arcaded courtyard is freely accessible to visitors and a pleasantly cool retreat from the heat of summer.

## PARQUE DE LAS CIENCIAS (O) *(*📍 *O)*

You can find everything you need to know about this interactive science museum in the 'Travel with Kids' chapter.

## PASEO DE LOS TRISTES ☀
(U E3) *(*📍 *e3)*

At the end of the Carrera del Darro on the southern edge of the Albaicín, this promenade juts out above the Río Darro. Take a seat at a terrace restaurant or just relax on a bench to enjoy the stunning views of the Alhambra, rising up on the opposite bank of the river. It is particularly impressive at night when the 'Red Fortress' is illuminated in sublime splendour. A great spot for romantics.

## PLAZA BIB-RAMBLA ● (U C4) *(*📍 *c4)*

Thanks to its central situation and the busy alleyways (such as Calle Zacatín) that radiate from it, this is the meeting place in the Old Town. In the middle of the square a fountain featuring a statue of Neptune gurgles away, surrounded by cafés and restaurants. There are two more attractive squares in the vicinity: *Plaza de la Romanilla*, with the new

Unmistakably Renaissance: the symmetrical façade of the Real Chancillería on Plaza Nueva

Federico García Lorca cultural centre, has a good view of the cathedral tower, while around the shady *Plaza de la Trinidad* are several tapas bars.

## PLAZA NUEVA (U C3) (🗺 c3)

An urban hub; access point for the Albaicín and Alhambra; a nightlife hotspot – the Plaza Nueva is many things. At the eastern end it merges with the *Plaza de Santa Ana*, which is dominated by the magnificent Renaissance façade of the former royal court, the *Real Chancillería*. Below Plaza Santa Ana, the smallest of Granada's three rivers, the Río Darro, disappears into an underground channel. In Moorish times a mosque stood on the site of the present-day church of *Santa Ana*.

## PLAZA DE LA UNIVERSIDAD (U B3) (🗺 b3)

The noise level of the students is just as much a feature of this bustling square in front of the Law Faculty as the church of Santos Justo y Pastor. The square merges with the *Plaza de la Encarnación,* an ideal place to take a break in one of the cafés.

## SACROMONTE ☀ (U F2) (🗺 f2)

Granada's picturesque district of Sacromonte is famous for its cave dwellings with their whitewashed entrances, its community of *gitanos* ('gypsies') and, of course, its flamenco. It is said that the first *gitanos* came to Granada as metalworkers with the army of the Catholic Monarchs. Sacromonte lies at the very edge of the city, high above the Darro valley, with gardens, side views of the Alhambra, remains of the old city wall and a proliferation of agaves and prickly pears. Washing hangs in front of the houses, but not everywhere is well tended, and obscure corners should be avoided at night. The route leads off Granada's beaten tourist tracks up to the INSIDER TIP *Museo Cuevas del Sacromonte (daily 10am–6pm, mid-March–mid-Oct until 8pm | Barranco de los Negros | www.sacromontegranada.com).* This folklore museum showcases a series of adjacent caves and explains the cave dwellers' way of life. The sleeping quarters are always at the back of the cave, the kitchen area at the very front. There are also storage areas for tools and food, and cave stables for donkeys and mules. The visit can be rounded off with a nice drink on the terrace of the museum bar.

Located in the solitude of the mountains just a short distance above the district is the *Abadía del Sacromonte (Tue–Sun 11am–1pm and 4pm–6pm, May–Oct 5pm–7.30pm | Camino del Sacromonte)*, an abbey dating from the 17th century. It has a small collection of art treasures as well as underground INSIDERTIP catacombs dating from the Roman period.

## FOOD & DRINK

Granada is one of the best places in the region for tapas bars (see 'Entertainment').

### HICURI ART VEGAN (U D4) *(ØD d4)*
Life can be so colourful – and the oriental seitan kebabs so tasty. The walls of this restaurant in the trendy Realejo quarter are covered in vivid murals and the purely vegetable-based cuisine is flamboyant too. *Closed Sun | Plaza Girones 4 | tel. 8 58 98 74 73 | www.restaurantehicuriart vegan.com | Budget–Moderate*

### TETERÍA AS-SIRAT (U C3) *(ØD c3)*
Moroccan mint tea from silver pots, alcohol-free cocktails and yoghurt shakes are the stars at this tea shop, which is one of the oldest in Granada. *Daily | Calle Caldererería Nueva 13*

### INSIDERTIP BOTÁNICO (U B3) *(ØD b3)*
This small restaurant opposite the Botanical Gardens operates according to the adage 'you eat with your eyes'. Asian-Japanese inspired dishes are presented correspondingly – each one a work of art

in its own right. *Daily | Calle Málaga 3 | tel. 9 58 27 15 98 | www.botanicocafe.es | Moderate*

### CARMEN DE SAN MIGUEL (U D4) *(ØD d4)*
Slightly hidden away near the Bermejas Towers of the Alhambra, this restaurant offers innovate Spanish cuisine. Good wine list and a lovely ☼ terrace. For the price-conscious diner there's a separate tapas bar including a INSIDERTIP tapas menu. *Closed Sun evening and June–Sept closed Sun | Plaza Torres Bermejas 3 | tel. 9 58 22 67 23 | www.carmensanmiguel. com | Moderate–Expensive*

### LAS TITAS (U D5) *(ØD d5)*
Café-restaurant in a lovely pavilion with INSIDERTIP relaxing terrace. Set in the park near the promenade on the Río Genil, it is off the beaten track. Inexpensive lunch menu. *Daily | Paseo de la Bomba | tel. 9 58 12 00 19 | kioskorestaurante lastitas.com | Budget–Moderate*

### AL PIE DE LA TORRE (U C3) *(ØD c3)*
Anyone looking for a place among locals won't go far wrong in this small restaurant right next to the cathedral. The food is 100 per cent Andalusian: as excellent tapas at the bar up front or from the menu in the back room. *Closed Mon | Calle Cárcel Baja 1 | tel. 9 58 28 38 48 | Budget–Moderate*

## SHOPPING

Jewellery, leather bags, fans and all the kitsch a tourist heart could desire is to be found in the Alcaicería between the cathedral and Plaza Bib Rambka in the alleyways of the former fabric market. The ascent to the Alhambra in the Cuesta de Gomérez is similarly colourful. A bazaarlike atmosphere reigns in the streets of

*Calderería Nueva* and *Calderería Vieja* at the foot of the *Albaicín*. Granada is famous for its handmade ceramics, inlays and guitars – for example at *Miguel Ángel Bellido (Paseo de las Palmas 1 | www.guitarreriabellido.com)* and *Guitarrería Gil de Avalle (Plaza de Realejo 15 | www.gildeavalle.com)*. There is a tradition of manufacturing (everyday) ceramics in Granada, characterised by shades of blue and green. You'll find a good selection, for example, at *Cerámica San Isidro (Plaza de San Isidro 5 | facebook: Cerámica San Isidro)* and *Cerámica los Arrayanes (Calle Alhóndiga 16 | ceramicalosarraya nes.com)*. The handmade inlays at *Artesanía del Arbol (Calle Paredes s/n, Carmen de San José | delarbol.net)* are also of high quality. The *Mercado de San*

which starts at the Puerta Real. Smarter boutiques and shoe shops are concentrated in the core of the Old Town, in the pedestrian zone around *Calle Mesones* (U B4) (*m b4*) and *Calle Zacatín* (U C4) (*m c4*).

## SPAS & BATHS

A number of ● Arab baths *(baños árabes)* in Granada are reviving the old Moorish traditions and providing a chance to relax in the city. They include the *Hammam Al-Andalus* (U D3) (*m d3*) (granada.hammamalandalus.com) in Calle Santa Ana 16 and the *Baños de Elvira* (U C3) (*m c3*) (www.banosdeelvira.es) in *Calle Arteaga 3*. Both offer their services from 35 euros.

Granada's flamenco bars are to be found in the Sacromonte district

*Agustín (Mon–Sat 9am–3pm | Plaza de San Agustín | www.mercadodesanagustin.com)* is first choice when it comes to filling cooking pots, pans and fruit bowls. The stomach doesn't have to stay empty either thanks to the street food stalls. There are several inexpensive clothes shops – as well as shoe shops – lining the *Calle Recogidas* (U A–B 4–5) (*m a–b 4–5*)

## ENTERTAINMENT

### EL BAR DE ERIC (U B3) (*m b3*)
Spain's famous drummer, Eric Jiménez, swaps his drumsticks for a wooden spoon. He once toured with the popular bands Los Evangelistas and Los Planetas, and the walls are adorned with mementos of this time: leather jackets, concert photographs

and tickets. Musicians often pop in for a drink after concerts. *Closed Mon | Calle Escuelas 8 | facebook: El Bar de Eric*

## FLAMENCO

Granada is considered the birthplace of flamenco. Music, song and the staccato click of the heels can be heard coming from the caves in the Gitano quarter *Sacromonte* every evening. You can usually choose between booking just the show with free drinks or also including dinner. You can also choose to be picked up from your hotel. Recommended stages include the *Cueva La Rocío (daily 8, 9, 10 and 11pm | entrance from 20 euros incl. drinks | Camino del Sacromonte 70 | tel. 9 58 22 71 29 | cuevalarocio.es)*, the *Cueva Venta El Gallo (daily 9.15 and 10.30pm | entrance from 26 euros incl. drinks | Barranco de los Negros 5 | tel. 9 58 22 84 76 | ventaelgallo.com)* and the *Cuevas Los Tarantos (daily 9 and 10.30pm | entrance from 26 euros incl. drinks | Camino de Sacromonte 9 | tel. 9 58 22 45 25 | cuevas lostarantos.com)*.

**INSIDER TIP ▶ SALA VIMAAMBI**
(U D3) *(ɰ d3)*

Small cultural centre with cinema, concerts, exhibitions and an artists' workshop, which promotes young talents. Their studio theatre stages the 'Raíz y Duende', a modern flamenco extravaganza including dance, music and poetry, but free of rehearsed folklore *(Fri/Sat 10pm | 15 euros incl. drinks). Cuesta de San Gregorio 30 | tel. 9 58 22 73 34 | www.vimaambi.com*

## TAPAS BARS ★ ●

In Granada tapas turns up next along with your drink, unsolicited and for free (vegetarians and vegans should 'warn' the barman in advance). A glass of beer or house wine costs an average of 2–2.50 euros including tapas. There are lots of stylish tapas bars clustered around *Plaza Nueva* (U C3) *(ɰ c3),* particularly in *Calle de Elvira,* where you'll find such traditional establishments as the *Antigua Bodega Castañeda (daily | Calle Elvira 5)* and the *Taberna Salinas* (lots of students) *(daily | Calle Elvira 13)*. Another

No longer possible today – *¡No fumar!* has long since been standard practice in Spanish bars

nice area for tapas bars is *Calle Navas* behind the *town hall* (U C4) (*[m] c4*), where places like *Las Copas (daily | no. 19)*, *La Chicotá (daily | no. 21)* and *Los Diamantes (daily | no. 28 | barlosdiamantes. com)* enjoy a good reputation among locals. An area less well known by outsiders but with several very pleasant haunts is the **INSIDER TIP** *Plaza Campo del Príncipe*. Those who like snails are sure to find happiness at *Los Altramuces* – the sauce in particular is incredibly aromatic *(closed Wed | Campo del Príncipe s/n)*.

## WHERE TO STAY

### HOTEL ALHAMBRA PALACE ⭘⭘
(U E4) (*[m] e4*)
Luxury hotel in an enormous neo-Moorish palace below the Alhambra plateau. Stunning views over the city. *126 rooms | Plaza Arquitecto García de Paredes 1 | tel. 9 58 22 14 68 | www.h-alhambrapalace. es | Expensive*

### LA ALMUNIA DEL VALLE ⭘⭘
(131 E4) (*[m] J4*)
If you want to get in the mood for a visit to the Sierra Nevada, you'd do well to choose this elegant boutique hotel in an old country house located in Monachil, 12 km/7.5 mi southwest of Granada. A walk in the terraced gardens affords you an unrivalled panoramic view of the 3482-m/11,421-ft high Mulhacén. The rooms are decorated with antique wall hangings; the restaurant serves up excellent cuisine. *15 rooms | Camino de la Umbría | tel. 9 58 30 80 10 | www.laal muniadelvalle.com | Moderate*

**INSIDER TIP** GAR-ANAT (U C4) (*[m] c4*)
Boutique hotel occupying a 17th-century mansion in the historic Jewish quarter of Realejo. The comfortable rooms lead off a courtyard, which has a 'Tree of Wish-

es', where you can hang a wish. Included in the price is the excellent breakfast buffet in the basement, as well as nice little gestures such as biscuits in the afternoon and water bottles at night. Television is available on request. Choose a room at the back! *15 rooms | Placeta de los Peregrinos 1 | tel. 9 58 22 55 28 | hotelgaranat. com | Moderate*

### EL LADRÓN DE AGUA (U D3) (*[m] d3*)
Small, friendly and atmospheric boutique hotel in a building dating from the 16th century on the edge of the Albaicín hill (not suitable for cars!). Various classes of room are available, all with a simple, refined elegance. As soon as you enter the covered courtyard with its wooden balustrades you feel welcome here. *15 rooms | Carrera del Darro 13 | tel. 9 58 21 50 40 | www.ladrondeagua.com | Moderate–Expensive*

### LANDAZURI (U D3) (*[m] d3*)
Reasonable prices and an excellent location between Plaza Nueva and the climb to the Alhambra make this an interesting proposition for low-budget travellers. En-suite or shared bathrooms. The same family also runs the neighbouring *Pensión Alfín (Cuesta de Gomérez 31 | tel. 9 58 22 81 72 | www.pensionalfin.com | Budget)* – four pleasant rooms at an amazingly low price. *17 rooms | Cuesta de Gomérez 24 | tel. 9 58 22 14 06 | www. pensionlandazuri.com | Budget*

### PARADOR DE GRANADA
(U E4) (*[m] e4*)
This hotel is one of the most popular and expensive in the parador chain: in a perfect location on the Alhambra plateau, housed in a former Franciscan monastery. Book well in advance! *40 rooms | Calle Real de la Alhambra | tel. 9 58 22 14 40 | www.parador.es | Expensive*

*In the town hall (Ayuntamiento) on Plaza del Carmen (U C4) (𝄞 c4) (tel. 9 58 24 82 80 | www.granadatur.com); Plaza de Santa Ana (U D3) (𝄞 d3) (tel. 9 58 57 52 02 | www.turgranada.es)*

## WHERE TO GO

**GUADIX (131 F3) (𝄞 K3–4)**

This town of 20,000 inhabitants, around 60 km/37 mi east of Granada, is like nowhere else in Spain, for here several thousand people still live in underground cave dwellings. Some of the caves have their own open-air patios where the washing is hung out to dry, others can only be accessed down steps. In the picturesque ⭐ *Barrio de Cuevas* quarter, the *Centro de Interpretación de las Cuevas (Mon–Fri 10am–2pm and 4pm–6pm, Sat 10am–2pm | entrance 2.60 euros | Plaza Padre Poveda | mcicuevasdeguadix.blog spot.com)*, provides an insight into underground architecture. The cave dwellings have an average size of 750 square feet and have no windows – natural light and ventilation come through the door. From the cave quarter, a short path leads from *Plaza Padre Poveda* to a ⭐ viewpoint *(mirador)* which provides the best views of Guadix, taking in the Alcazaba (Moorish fortress), the cathedral tower and the bizarre-looking cliffs in the background. A walk round the viewpoint takes you directly above the rooftops of the caves, as indicated by those telltale white symbols of the town: the chimneys. A further cave, the *Cueva La Alcazaba,* lies below the castle on *Calle San Miguel*. It contains the pottery museum, the *Museo de la Alfarería (Mon–Fri 10am–1.30pm and 4pm–7pm, 5pm–8.30pm in summer, Sat–Sun 11am–2pm)*. In contrast to the modest caves, the *Cathedral* is full of religious pomp and splendour with a bombastic Baroque facade. Begun in 1492, the edifice took more than 300 centuries to complete. If the caves have aroused your curiosity, you can try staying in one of the INSIDER TIP cave hotels such as the *Cuevas Pedro Antonio de Alarcón (23 apartments | Barriada San*

# FEDERICO GARCÍA LORCA

Federico García Lorca (1898–1936) was one of Spain's greatest poets and dramatists, and tragedies such as 'The House of Bernarda Alba' are still performed both at home and abroad. Born into affluent circumstances in the village of Fuente Vaqueros 18 km/11 mi northwest of Granada, he always maintained a close bond with his home. In Huerta de San Vicente, his summer home in Granada, he wrote the theatre classics 'Yerma' and 'Blood Wedding'. Lorca's homosexuality and outspoken liberal views brought him enemies, and ultimately a tragic end: at the beginning of the Spanish Civil War in August 1936 he was captured and shot near Granada by right-wing rebels loyal to General Franco. In Fuente Vaqueros, his birthplace *Casa Natal (Tue–Sun 10am, 11am, noon, 1pm, also July–Sept Tue–Sat 2pm, Oct–March 4pm and 5pm, April–June 5pm and 6pm | Calle Poeta Federico García Lorca 4 | www.patron atogarcialorca.org)* can be visited as part of a guided tour.

On the summit of Pico de Veleta: on a clear day you can see Africa

*Torcuato | tel. 958664986 | www.cuevaspedroantonio.es | Budget–Moderate).* Information: *Plaza de la Constitución 15 | tel. 958662804 | www.guadix.es*

## SIERRA NEVADA ★ ●

(132 A–C 4–5) (*J–L4*)

Rising majestically within sight of Granada, the Sierra Nevada is the highest mountain range on the Iberian Peninsula. It is crowned by *Mulhacén* (3482 m/ 11,421 ft and *Pico de Veleta* (3392 m/ 11,129 ft). In winter, the upper reaches are covered in snow and ice, otherwise the range is characterised by jagged ridges of crag and scree. Most of the mountainous area is under protection as a 332-square-mile nature reserve. More than 2000 plant species have been documented, and with a bit of luck you should see golden eagles and ibex here. The easiest way to reach the Sierra Nevada is to take the well-surfaced A395 mountain road, which winds its way up into the high mountains for about 35 km/22 mi southeast of Granada. On the way you'll pass olive trees, then pine trees and small gorges. The higher you go, the bigger the mountain panorama, until you get to *Pradollano,* the Sierra Nevada's ski resort at an altitude of 2100 m/ 6890 ft, with attendant shops, ski schools, restaurants, cafés, bars and nightclubs. Outside the ski season it all looks a bit forlorn. You can continue your journey along the A395 beyond Pradollano, until it stops at the 2500 m/8202 ft sign and a car park. From there, hikers set off into the high mountains.

Towards the south, the Sierra Nevada drops to the foothills of the Alpujarra, a scenic area scattered with villages. Here, too, a road from the south approaches the mountains via Lanjarón and Capileira, but the ascent is closed to private vehicles for reasons of environmental protection. Instead, between the months of May and October – and depending on the weather and latest regulations – a shuttle bus takes visitors from Capileira at 1420 m/4659 ft to the 2700-m/ 8858-ft *Mirador de Trevélez*, which provides access to some magnificent hiking country. Information from *Nevadensis (tel. 958763127 | www.nevadensis.com)* on *Plaza de la Libertad* in *Pampaneira,* which also arranges INSIDER TIP guided hiking tours (see also description of a trip through the landscape of the Alpujarra in the 'Discovery Tours' chapter).

# COSTA DEL SOL AROUND MÁLAGA

In terms of resorts, the eastern and central Sun Coast encompass everything from the heavily built-up and brash to the more modest and laid-back. Popular bases include Torremolinos and Nerja, while the marina of Benalmádena is one of the nicest in Spain. Right in the middle of the coast is the engaging city of Málaga, the birthplace of Pablo Picasso. The coastal strip rises to totally unspoiled landscapes, complete with olive groves, vineyards and white villages. As far as the beaches are concerned, the picture is mixed: there are small ones, sometimes divided into several bays as at Nerja, and long continuous beaches such as the one in Torremolinos. But there are no secret, hidden-away places any more; in summer all the beaches are packed.

# MÁLAGA

MAP ON P. 134/135
(130 B–C5) *(Ⅲ G5)* **Founded by the Phoenicians, this city of 570,000 souls won't inspire love at first sight.**
But beyond the rings of high-rises, port facilities and constant drone of traffic, there is enduring evidence of a long and eventful past. Today, the city is famous for its museums, including the renowned Picasso Museum, and is a popular cruise port.

## SIGHTSEEING

**ALCAZABA** ☀ (135 E2) *(Ⅲ I2)*
Built on a hill rising above the Old Town, the Alcazaba was the stronghold of

Between the high life and mountain air: the heart of the Costa del Sol, where plane-loads of northern sun-worshipers land

🏙 **WHERE TO START?**

The best point of reference is **Plaza de la Marina (135 E1–2)** *(🗺 I1–2)* where you'll also find the tourist office. Bus and rail travellers arrive at Estación Maria Zambrano. From there it's a 20-minute walk into the city or 10 minutes by bus (e.g. 20 and C2). Car parks near the centre include Plaza de la Marina and Calle Santa Ana.

Moorish governors from the 11th century. It is the best-preserved fortress palace in Spain, with typical Moorish features such as horseshoe arches still intact. While some of the restoration is over the top and hibiscus bushes, bougainvillea and pools have softened the military severity of the complex, it's worth climbing up for the views over the port, with its cranes and ships, the pleasant Paseo del Parque and the Cathedral. The vista also takes in the bullring. A good-value combination ticket is available for the

Alcazaba and the Castillo de Gibralfaro. *Daily 9am–6pm, summer until 8pm | Calle de la Alcazabilla 2*

## CASTILLO DE GIBRALFARO ★ ⊰⊱
(135 F2) (*m2*)

Connected to the Alcazaba by a double defensive wall, the Moors' upper castle dates from the 14th century. It functioned as a lookout post over the city and also boasted considerable firepower. Today

towers that were planned was built. In the cavernous interior, gigantic columns rise to the 40-m-/130-ft-high vaults. The dimensions, the distance between the altar and the pews, as well as the lavish decor and oil paintings in the various chapels don't exactly make for a contemplative atmosphere. But the choir stalls, by Pedro de Mena, are a sculptural masterpiece. Typical of Spain, the organ has horizontal pipes in order to improve the

Despite 250 years' construction, Málaga's cathedral has never really been completed

the fort is a peaceful island of greenery, where you can stroll along the much restored crenellated battlements and enjoy great views over the tops of pine trees to the city, coast and hinterland. *Daily 9am–6pm, summer until 8pm*

## CATEDRAL DE LA ENCARNACIÓN
(135 D2) (*j2*)

Málaga's cathedral exudes strength and power. Built on the site of a former mosque, its construction spanned more than 250 years (1528–1782), although it was never actually completed. It is known locally as La Manquita, 'the one-armed one', because only one of the two

acoustics and to prevent dust getting in. *Mon–Thu 9am–6pm, Fri 10am–6pm, Sat 10am–5pm | entrance 5 euros (incl. cathedral museum Ars Málaga in the neighbouring bishop's palace), tour of the roof 6 euros, combined ticket 10 euros, Mon–Thu 9am–10am free | Calle Molina Lario 9 | malagacatedral.com*

## INSIDER TIP CENTRE POMPIDOU MÁLAGA (135 F3) (*m3*)

Opened in 2015, the offshoot of the Centre Pompidou in Paris houses more than 70 works from the 20th and 21st centuries by such illustrious artists as Max Ernst, René Magritte, Frida Kahlo and

Francis Bacon. In addition to the permanent exhibition, there are temporary shows every year. The exhibition hall – a glass cube clad in colourful squares – on the Muelle Uno promenade at the harbour can be spotted from afar. *Wed–Mon 9.30am–8pm | entrance 7 euros, special exhibition 4 euros, combined ticket 9 euros, Sun from 4pm free | Pasaje Doctor Carrillo Casaux | centrepompidou-malaga.eu*

### CENTRO DE ARTE CONTEMPORÁNEO (CAC) ● (134 B4) (*∅ h4*)

Housed in the former Rationalist-style wholesale market, this is a great venue for contemporary art, with lovely big display spaces. The *Colección Permanente* also features works by Louise Bourgeois, Thomas Hirschhorn, Damien Hirst and Olafur Eliasson. Changing exhibitions supplement the offering, often drawing on the museum's own stock. Free admission. *Summer Tue–Sun 10am–2pm and 5pm–9pm, otherwise Tue–Sun 10am–8pm | Calle Alemania | cacmalaga.org*

### INSIDER TIP▶ COLECCIÓN DEL MUSEO RUSO (0) (*∅ 0*)

The former tobacco factory re-opened its doors in 2015 as a branch of the state museum of St Petersburg. The permanent show includes Russian art from the 16th century to the avant-garde: icons, portraits, landscapes, historic avant-garde and Socialist Realism. Big names such as Wassily Kandinsky and Marc Chagall are also represented. *Tue–Sun 9.30am–8pm | Av. Sor Teresa Prat 15 | www.coleccionmuseoruso.es*

### MUSEO ALBORANIA ●
(135 E3) (*∅ l3*)

Take the plunge and dip into the underwater world to find out about the Costa del Sol's typical marine plants and creatures – right on the Muelle Uno promenade at the harbour. Learn something about the sea with a view of the same. *Mid-Sept–June daily 10.30am–2pm, Thu–Sun also 4.30pm–6.30pm, July–mid-Sept daily 11am–2pm and 5pm–8pm | entrance 7, children (aged 4–17) 5 euros | museo alborania.es*

### MUSEO AUTOMOVILÍSTICO MÁLAGA
(0) (*∅ 0*)

Incorporating part of the old tobacco factory, this fascinating museum contains beautiful vintage motorcars from all over the world. It takes you on a journey through time, as the aesthetic and technical development of the motorcar is revealed. *Tue–Sun 10am–7pm | Av. Sor Teresa Prat 15 | www.museoautomovil malaga.com*

## MUSEO CARMEN THYSSEN
(134 C2) *(ꕥ j2)*

A mix of old and modern architecture provides the setting for this notable art museum. The exhibits in the permanent collection include a 'Santa Marina' by the master Francisco de Zurbarán (1598–1664) and works by Spanish painters from the 19th and 20th centuries, including Guillermo Gómez Gil, Ignacio Zuloaga and Julio Romero de Torres, who concentrated on more everyday scenes and themes. There are also temporary exhibitions. *Tue–Sun 10am–8pm | 10 euros, 2.30pm–4pm 6 euros | Plaza Carmen Thyssen | carmenthyssenmalaga.org*

## MUSEO INTERACTIVO DE LA MÚSICA
(135 D1) *(ꕥ k1)*

In certain parts of this interactive music museum the signs probably should read 'Please *do* touch'! Located in the Palacio del Conde de las Navas, the museum's several hundred instruments take visitors on a journey through the musical traditions of many different countries and periods. Remains of the old city wall are integrated into the museum. *End June–start Sept Mon 10.30am–4pm, Tue–Sun 10.30am–7.30pm, otherwise Mon 10am–4pm, Tue–Sun 10am–7pm | 5 euros, children (aged over 6) 3 euros*

## MUSEO PICASSO ★ ●
(135 E2) *(ꕥ l2)*

It was the wish of Pablo Picasso (1881–1973) that a representative collection of his work be displayed in the city of his birth (Picasso's family lived in Mál-

aga until 1891) – and that makes Málaga a prime address when it comes to art. In the Renaissance Buenavista Palace the world of the great artist, master of a variety of styles, techniques and materials, is revealed – with early and late works, oil paintings, sketches and ceramics all on show. Pictures of bulls betray his Spanish soul, portraits of women his passions. Exhibits in the permanent collection include, among others: *Búho sobre una silla* ('Owl Sitting on a Chair'), *Jacqueline sentada* ('Seated Jacqueline') and *Naturaleza muerta con cráneo y tres erizos* ('Still Life with Skull and Three Hedgehogs'). The works, which range from his earliest to last creative phase, are priceless. The INSIDERTIP▶ museum café is the perfect place to take a break, and the basement of the former palace holds a surprise that has nothing at all to do with Picasso: Roman and Phoenician remains, some of them over 2500 years old. On the website there's a link for advance ticket booking. There's also a space for temporary exhibitions (special ticket or combined entry with the permanent collection). Free admission on Sundays after 6pm or until the museum becomes overcrowded – whichever comes first. *Daily 10am–6pm, March–June and Sept/Oct until 7pm, July/Aug until 8pm | permanent exhibition incl. audio guide (also in English) 8 euros, temporary exhibition 6.50 euros, combined ticket 12 euros, Sun free entrance for the last two hours | Calle de San Agustín 8 | www.museopicassomalaga.org*

## MUSEO DEL VIDRIO Y CRISTAL
(135 D1) *(ꕥ k1)*

This remarkable glass museum is located in an 18th-century palace. Its collection comprises around 2000 items from various epochs. It's worth taking a guided tour. *Tue–Sun 11am–7pm | 6 euros incl.*

Plaza de la Merced, where a bronze statue of Picasso stands in front of his birthplace

guided tour | Plazuela del Santísimo Cristo de la Sangre 2 | museovidrioycristalmalaga.com

### PLAZA DE LA MERCED

(135 E1–2) (*m l1–2*)

An obelisk in the centre, lots of pigeons, benches and cafés – impressions of one of Málaga's main squares, which is also the location of Pablo Picasso's birthplace. The Picasso Foundation runs the *Museo Casa Natal de Picasso (daily 9.30am–8pm | fundacionpicasso.malaga.eu)*, a modest museum in which photos recall the little Pablo, and temporary exhibitions the great Picasso. Free admission on Sundays.

### SOHO MÁLAGA

(134 C3–4) (*m j3–4*)

Residents and shop owners breathe cultural life under the banner 'Soho Málaga' into this quarter between the harbour, Río Guadalmedina and Alameda Principal. This also embraces the sister project Málaga Art Urban Soho (MAUS), which organises theatre productions, photography competitions, swap meets and workshops. The focus is on street art, so there's bags of graffiti on the walls, including by such internationally famous names as Faith 47, ROA, DALeast, D*Face and Obey. *soho.malaga.eu, www.soho mlg.com*

### TEATRO ROMANO (135 E2) (*m l2*)

The remains of this Roman theatre are at the entrance to the Alcazaba. It dates from the 1st century AD and would have been in operation until the 3rd century. In the Middle Ages, the Moors used the site as a quarry for building the Alcazaba, and it was only rediscovered in the mid-20th century, during excavation work. *Tue 10am–6pm, Wed–Sat 9am–7pm, May–Sept until 8.30pm, Sun 10am–4pm | entrance free | Calle de la Alcazabilla 8*

## FOOD & DRINK

### EL JARDÍN (135 D2) (*m k2*)

This traditional eatery by the cathedral is a mix of café and restaurant. It serves simple dishes and salads, but also classier fare, such as braised oxtail or marinated partridge. Musical evenings too; usually tango on Thursdays and flamenco on Fridays and Saturdays. *Closed Sun evening | Calle Cañón 1 | tel. 9 52 22 04 19 | www.el jardinmalaga.com | Budget–Moderate*

### RESTAURANTE JOSÉ CARLOS GARCÍA
**(135 F3) (Ⓜ m3)**

The perfect example of sophisticated, modern Andalusian cuisine on a small square at the harbour comes at a price (degustation menu from 140 euros). But the star chef José Carlos García also runs the classic *Café de Paris* just around the corner *(closed Sun evening and Mon | Calle Vélez-Málaga 8 | tel. 9 52 22 50 43 | www.rcafedeparis.com | Moderate–Expensive)*, where the food is almost as good, but cheaper. *Closed Sun/Mon | Plaza de la Capilla/Muelle Uno | tel. 9 52 00 35 88 | www.restaurantejcg.com |Expensive*

**INSIDER TIP SPAIN FOOD SHERPAS**

The Spain Food Sherpas operate very special tours, taking visitors by the hand and leading them to shops, restaurants and tapas bars that they would never find without their aid. Or you can visit a workshop for a demonstration of how to make authentic tapas yourself. *tel. 9 52 21 03 07 | www.spainfoodsher pas.com*

## SHOPPING

There's a huge selection of boutiques and shoe shops around *Calle Puerta del Mar, Calle Nueva* and *Calle Marqués de Larios* **(134–135 C–D 2–3) (Ⓜ j–k 2–3)**. There's also a big choice of shopping centres such as the *Málaga Plaza* **(134 B2) (Ⓜ h2)** *(Calle Armengual de la Mota 12 | www.malagaplaza.com)* and *Larios Centro* **(134 A3) (Ⓜ g3)** *(Av. de la Aurora 25 | www.larioscentro.com)*.

## BEACHES

Málaga, a city of half a million people with a busy industrial area, is hardly the ideal seaside holiday destination. The 14 km/8.5 mi of rather unattractive city beaches, beginning east of the harbour basin with the *Playa de la Malagueta* and continuing eastwards as far as the marina of *El Candado*, are best left to the locals.

## LEISURE & SPORT

Themed tours by bike are offered by *Málaga Bike Tours & Rentals* **(135 D3) (Ⓜ k3)** *(Calle Trinidad Grund 4 | tel. 9 51 13 83 49 | www.malagabiketours.eu)* and include a 'Tapas Bike Tour' and an alternative 'Off the Tourist Track Ride'. Bikes for hire too.

## ENTERTAINMENT

The tapas bars on Plaza de la Merced, around Calle Granada and on the new harbour are busy deep into the night. The atmosphere in *Centro de Arte Flamenco Kelipé (Wed, Fri, Sat 9 pm | 25 euros incl. drinks | Muro de la Puerta Nueva 10 | tel. 6 92 82 98 85 | kelipe.net)* is also very authentic. Event listings can be found at *www.malakao.es* and *fundacionmalaga. com* (also in English).

## WHERE TO STAY

**DON PACO (134 A5) (Ⓜ g5)**
Comfortable hotel in a busy area near the railway and bus stations. *31 rooms | Calle Salitre 53 | tel. 9 52 31 90 08 | www.hotel-donpaco.com | Budget*

**NH MÁLAGA (134 B3) (Ⓜ h3)**
Comfortable 4-star hotel, located near the city next to a bridge across the dry riverbed of the Rio Guadalmedina. It's

part of the NH chain. INSIDER TIP Good breakfast buffet. *133 rooms | Calle San Jacinto 2 | tel. 952 07 13 23 | www.nh-hoteles.es | Moderate*

**PETIT PALACE PLAZA** (135 D2) (*Ø k2*)
Located in the heart of the city, with thoughtful touches; each room has a computer. *66 rooms | Calle Nicasio 3 | tel. 952 22 21 32 | www.hthoteles.com | Moderate*

## INFORMATION

*Plaza de la Marina 11* (135 D3) (*Ø k3*) | *tel. 951 92 60 20 | www.malagaturismo.com*

## WHERE TO GO

**ANTEQUERA** ⭐ (130 B4) (*Ø F4*)
Dolmen and churches, a nice Old Town and a Moorish castle – these are reasons enough for a detour to Antequera (pop. 41,000). The around 4500-year-old *Menga* and *Viera* dolmen are part of an archaeological complex on the way into town from Málaga (on the A-7282). The roughly 700 years younger dolmen *El Romeral* is on the A-7283, further northeast of the city centre *(visiting times for all three dolmen Tue–Sat April–June 9am-9pm, July–mid-Sept 9am–3pm and 8pm–10pm, mid-Sept–March 9am–6pm, Sun 9am–3pm, | EU citizens ● entrance free, otherwise 1.50 euros | www.museosdeandalucia.es/web/conjuntoarqueologicodolmenesdeantequera).* Inside Menga is a large, atmospherically lit chamber with enormous roof slabs and supports.

In the historic district of *Coso Viejo,* you can stroll across Plaza de San Sebastián, which has a church of the same name, its tower crowned by a weathervane with the figure of an angel (El Angelote), and Plaza Coso Viejo, where there is an equestrian statue of King Ferdinand I, who wrested Antequera from the Moors in 1410. Dominating the hill above the Old Town is the restored Moorish castle, the ✲ *Alcazaba (daily 10am–6pm | 6 euros, Tue 2pm–6pm entrance free).* From there, you'll get the best view over Antequera's white sea of houses, of the surrounding olive groves, the Sierra de Chimenea and

Viera dolmen in Antequera: the megalithic burial chamber was rediscovered in the 20th century

the enormous isolated crag of limestone called La Peña de los Enamorados, or 'The Lovers' Leap', which juts out of the plain. On the plateau, there is also the Renaissance church *Real Colegiata de Santa María,* which now serves as an exhibition space *(Mon–Sat 10.30am–5.30pm, Sun 10.30am–3pm | 3 euros).* The cooks in the hotel restaurant *Arte de Cozina,* with a charming patio in an old town palace, also see their job as an art form *(daily | Calle Calzada 27 | tel. 9 52 84 00 14 | arte decozina.com | Moderate).*

## INSIDER TIP CAMINITO DEL REY
(130 A4) (*ℳ F5*)

The once dilapidated via ferrata across the *Paraje Natural Desfiladero de los Gaitanes* gorge was opened again in 2015 after many years of renovation work. The route was originally built around 100 m above the river at the beginning of the 20th century to enable workers to access the hydroelectric power station, Sociedad Hidroeléctrica del Chorro. The new *caminito* has been re-created on the original trail using wooden planks which are anchored to the rock face with metal struts. This makes the gorge, which reaches depths of up to 400 m, manageable for practically anyone. But you need to have a good head for heights here, as parts of the boardwalk are constructed out of glass panels. In total, the route is almost 8 km/5 mi long; of which around 1.5 km are on the actual boardwalk. The opening of the visitors centre on Puerto de las Atalayas (junction of MA-5403/ Ctra. de los Embalses) is planned for 2019 *(Tue–Sat Nov–Holy Week 9.30am–3pm, otherwise to 5pm | entrance 10 euros | tel. 9 02 78 73 25 | www.caminitodel rey.info | entry from 8 years old | parking at El Mirador restaurant and at the visitors centre, return trip to car park by shuttle bus | buying tickets far in advance is recommended as only a limited number of hikers are permitted every 30 min).*

## COMARES (130 C5) (*ℳ G5*)

The white village lies on a rocky outcrop in the Axarquía, 40 km/25 mi northeast of Málaga. A ☀ *viewing platform* offers a fantastic view. The panorama can be

For a cool head and sure foot: the spectacular via ferrata, Caminito del Rey

enjoyed in comfort from the restaurant terrace of Balcón de Comares, an oil mill that has been converted into a hotel and museum INSIDER TIP *El Molino de los Abuelos (daily | Plaza de la Axarquía 2 | tel. 9 52 50 94 06 | balcondecomares.word press.com | Moderate).* Your path up through the winding alleyways is sure to lead you to the white cemetery on the former castle grounds. It's more than likely you will hear music while exploring: Comares is also known for honouring the tradition of Verdiales, an archetypal form of flamenco with guitar, violin, tambourine, dancers and singers.

### INSIDER TIP LOBO PARK ☺
**(130 B4) (𝄢 F5)**

Their graceful movement, their lonely, penetrating eyes, their clear hierarchy in the pack – wolves! You will encounter some 30 of these magnificent creatures in this wolf park to the southwest of Antequera (60 km/37 mi northwest of Málaga, approach via Álora or Antequera). The enclosures cover a total area of 25 acres and are dotted with shrubs and stone oaks. There are timber wolves from Canada, as well as Alaskan, Iberian and European wolves and a she-wolf from Alaska. Daniel and Alexandra, the German couple who own the park, give the animals as much space as possible in which to play, hunt and relax. The visit takes the form of a 90-minute guided tour. Paths around the enclosures and individual platforms allow visitors to observe the wolves' natural behaviour. Most of the wolves were born in the park and are used to having people around them. There is also a petting farm with pigs, sheep and goats. From May to October (and on nights of the full moon in winter) you can experience a 'Wolf Howl Night'; for reservations *tel. 9 52 03 11 07. Thu–Tue 10am–6pm, guided tours usu-*

*ally 11am, 1pm, 3pm and 4.30pm | entrance 11 euros, children (aged 3–12) 7 euros, evening tour (3.5 hours) 25, children 17 euros | Ctra. A 343 Antequera–Álora km 16 | tel. 9 52 03 11 07 | www.lobo park.com*

### MONTES DE MÁLAGA
**(130 B–C5) (𝄢 G5)**

This mountainous region just north of Málaga is swathed in dense forest, dominated by the Aleppo pines that were planted here in the 1930s in a major programme of reforestation. The hills themselves reach heights of up to 1032 m/3385 ft. To get there, from the northeastern fringes of the city take the narrow ✂ A 7000 country road, which runs through the park from south to north in the direction of Colmenar, and along its initial stages provides fine views back down to Málaga and the sea. Along the route there are turn-offs to the INSIDER TIP *Hotel Cortijo La Reina (36 rooms | tel. 9 51 90 09 39 | hotelcortijola reina.com | Budget–Moderate)* and to the historic winery of *Lagar de Torrijos,* where a small trekking area begins.

### EL TORCAL DE ANTEQUERA ★
**(130 B4) (𝄢 F5)**

Some 50 km/31 mi north on the way to Antequera you come upon a stunning, enchanted landscape. The karst mountain range is Andalusia's most bizarre nature reserve, a fairy-tale world and geological oddity. It's easy to reach the start and end point of the walk, the car park at the *Centro de Visitantes (daily 10am–5pm, April–Sept until 7pm | torcal deantequera.com)* with café-restaurant. Follow the yellow *Ruta Amarilla,* which in places is identical to the shorter, green *Ruta Verde,* to immerse yourself fully in the mountain world. Despite being short, only 3 km/1.8 mi, this hike is a great experience! It requires the appropriate

Nerja: antiquated charm, not least thanks to a lack of hotel bunkers

footwear, however, as the paths can become slippy, depending on the weather. Back at the visitor centre, it's just a few steps to the unrivalled viewing point, ⚡ *Mirador las Ventanillas,* to round off your outing.

# NERJA

(131 D5) *(⌘ H5)* **Small beaches, a pleasant climate, attractive squares and atmospheric alleyways, plus splendid views of the coast and mountains – this is the appeal of Nerja (pop. 21,000) at the eastern end of the Costa del Sol.**

Nerja has developed from a fishing village into an attractive little holiday town. Sure, there are some new developments inland, but the local topography, with its cliffs and beaches enclosed by rocky headlands, has prevented unbridled development along the coast. In typical Andalusian style, locals love

a good party. Whether it's Carnival, the midsummer celebrations in June, celebrations to honour the Virgen del Carmen on 16 July or during the main *feria* in October.

## SIGHTSEEING

### BALCÓN DE EUROPA ★ ● ⚡

This is Nerja's showpiece, and together with the palm-lined promenade behind, it's a favourite spot for a stroll or for a rest on one of the benches. Spain's King Alfonso XII thought up the name 'Balcony of Europe' when he visited Nerja in 1885 and here, high above the water, took in all that sea air. Built on a vertical cliff and the remains of a hardly recognisable medieval fortification, the Balcón de Europa provides one of the most beautiful viewpoints in Andalusia. There's a bronze statue of Alfonso XII standing on his 'balcony', which separates the beaches of Calahonda and El Salón.

## CUEVA DE NERJA ⭐

Stone cascades, curtains, throws, columns – these are just some of the intriguing formations that will capture your imagination. Are they wrinkled old women, cacti, goblins, rats' heads in profile, the baleen of a whale, or organ pipes? The spectacular Caves of Nerja have all the many features typical of a dripstone cave. Each year, several hundred thousand visitors come to explore the caverns, and in high season it can get very crowded. An auditorium has been built into one of the halls – in July it is the setting for a dance and music festival.

Rediscovered in 1959, the caves were in use as long as 25,000 years ago. The caves lie to the east of the town, with the entrance to the car park well signposted. *Daily 9.30am–3.30pm, July/Aug until 6pm | entrance 10 euros | www.cuevadenerja.es*

## MUSEO DE NERJA

The local museum also includes an archaeological department showing finds from the famous caves. *Daily 10am–2pm and 4pm–6.30pm, July/Aug until 8pm | Plaza de España*

## FOOD & DRINK

### MARISQUERÍA LA MARINA

Fish and seafood set the tone on the menu. During the week there's a cheap lunchtime menu. Sit on the spacious terrace in summer. *Daily | Plaza de la Marina | tel. 9 52 52 12 99 | Budget–Moderate*

### JULIES & VALERI'S

The atmosphere here is always fantastic and the English-Cuban hosts will make you feel at home immediately. The vegetarian tapas are also superb. *Daily | Plaza Balcón de Europa | tel. 6 33 72 83 16 | Budget–Moderate*

## SHOPPING

Street markets are held in the Urbanización Flamingo every Tuesday and Sunday morning.

## BEACHES

Nerja is distinctive for its mix of rocky coast and small beaches, to the west and east of the Balcón de Europa. The largest beach, ⚡ *Playa de Burriana,* lies further

# THE HEART OF THE STORM

'Se vende' – for sale: such signs remain a constant reminder of the seemingly never-ending crisis in Spain. You see them on houses, apartments, pubs, restaurants and even yachts. But nobody wants to buy them. The economic crisis led to the collapse of the property sector. Experts had long warned this was on the cards, but optimists thought the boom times would last forever. Short-sighted construction policies were based on speculation and corruption. Come what may, ever more new settlements – *urbanizaciones* – were created, often in neo-Moorish style (and using substandard materials), and ever further from the saturated development along the coast. The result has been corporate bankruptcies, people desperately wanting to sell with no one to sell to, empty properties, half-completed schemes and ghost developments.

to the east: coarse-grained sand, some restaurants on the adjacent Paseo Marítimo Antonio Mercero, showers, children's play area, pedal boats, nice views inland and along the coast to the east.

## SPORTS & ACTIVITIES

You can book diving courses with *Buceo Costa Nerja (Playa de Burriana | tel. 9 52 52 86 10 | www.nerjadiving.com).*

## ENTERTAINMENT

Nerja's nightlife is centred on the *Calle de la Gloria* and around *Plaza Tutti-Frutti.* There's a colourful programme of

theatre, dance and concert performances at the *Centro Cultural Villa de Nerja (Calle Granada 45 | tel. 9 52 52 38 63).*

## WHERE TO STAY

### BALCÓN DE EUROPA ⚘

Large high-rise hotel overlooking Playa de Caletilla and right next to the *Balcón de Europa* – what a location! *108 rooms | Paseo Balcón de Europa 1 | tel. 9 52 52 08 00 | www.hotelbalconeuropa. com | Expensive*

### PLAZA CAVANA

Centrally located 3-star hotel with small terrace and pool. *39 rooms | Plaza Cavana 10 | tel. 9 52 52 40 00 | www.hotel plazacavana.com | Moderate*

## INFORMATION

*Calle Carmen 1/Bajos del Ayuntamiento | tel. 9 52 52 15 31 | www.nerja.es*

## WHERE TO GO

### CALA DE MARO (131 D5) (⌀ H5)

This pleasant, approx. 200-m-long sandy bay a good 5 km/3 mi east of Nerja belongs already to the neighbouring town of Maro, where a winding road is signed down to the car park.

### CÓMPETA (131 D5) (⌀ H5)

It is a winding road indeed that leads up from the coast to Cómpeta (pop. 4000). Situated at an altitude of 630 m/2066 ft, some 20 km/13 mi northwest of Nerja at the foot of the Sierra Tejeda and Sierra Almijara, it cultivates its image as a large white village and wine centre. The local dessert wine is called *Vino de Cómpeta;* the vineyards are spread across steep terraces surrounding the village. The mountains, the huddle of white houses

# LOW BUDGET

In Nerja there's a selection of cheap guesthouses along *Calle Pintada*, including the *Hostal Plaza Cantarero (10 rooms | Calle Pintada 117 | tel. 9 52 52 87 28 | www.hostalplazacan tarero.com)* and the *Hostal Nerja Sol (21 rooms | Calle Pintada 54 | tel. 9 52 52 21 21 | www.hostalnerjasol. com).* In high season, you can get a double room for around 50 euros, in low season 30 euros.

From Málaga airport, the C1 suburban train line *(Renfe Cercanías)* is a really cheap, fast and comfortable alternative, both for getting into the city and to Torremolinos, Benalmádena and Fuengirola. *www.renfe.com/ viajeros/cercanias/malaga*

In Málaga, admission to the Alcazaba and Castillo de Gibralfaro is free on Sunday after 2pm.

Flower-filled steps, alleyways and squares: the white village of Frigiliana

tumbling down the slopes, the alleyways and the 37-m-/121-ft-high tower of the Iglesia Parroquial make Cómpeta a quiet but attractive place. Life here carries on at a leisurely pace; funerals and weddings are major social events. You can get tapas and bottles of Cómpeta wine at the *Museo del Vino (closed Mon | Av. de la Constitución | tel. 9 52 55 33 14 | Budget)*, a mixture of shop, bar and restaurant. *www.turismocompeta.es*

### FRIGILIANA ★ ● ↝ (131 D5) (*∅ H5*)
The white village is spread across the foothills of the Sierra Tejeda and Sierra Almijara just 6 km/4 mi north of Nerja. A good place to start exploring is the Plaza del Ingenio, where the *El Ingenio sugar factory*, originally built as a mansion, still produces sugar cane syrup *(miel de caña)*. Frigiliana rises over several levels up to the pleasant square in front of the church of San Antonio. Typical of the alleyways are the hanging flowerpots, planters placed next to the entrances,

looping electric cables, and the ubiquitous bougainvillea. Ceramic plates on the walls have pictures and text describing the fall of Frigiliana castle and other events from Moorish times. Information: *Cuesta del Apero 8 | tel. 9 52 53 42 61 | www.turismofrigiliana.es*

● ↝ INSIDER TIP *La Posada Morisca (12 rooms | Calle Loma de la Cruz | tel. 9 52 53 41 51 | www.laposadamoriscacom | Moderate–Expensive)*, a beautiful country house with a pool and lovely views over the olive groves and the sea, lies 3 km/1.8 mi outside the village on the road to Torrox. If you go for it you'll be opting for an oasis of tranquillity!

### TORRE DEL MAR (131 D5) (*∅ H5*)
The extensive sunbathing areas, with sun loungers and parasols, are the main attraction of this rather sterile coastal resort 20 km/13 mi to the west of Málaga. The 2-km-/1.2-mi-long beach with its coarse-grained black sand is called *Playa de Poniente*.

# TORRE-MOLINOS

**(130 B6)** *(⚏ F6)* **A three-hour flight to Málaga airport, followed by a 10-minute transfer, and there you are, right in the thick of things!**

Those coming here in summer generally know what they want. And it's certainly not culture! Fun, sun and alcohol is what it's all about, and there are more than enough bars where you can get tanked up before going off to the clubs and discos. Torremolinos (pop. 68,000) is a holiday option for a diverse range of people from gays to families. It is the archetypal package-tour destination: with 50,000 beds, it prides itself on having 40 per cent of the total capacity of the entire Costa del Sol. In view of this, it looks pretty much as you might expect, with large, ugly developments scarring the landscape. The touristic appeal of the town lies in its long and immaculate sandy beaches, its handsome promenades and some 300 restaurants. The main thoroughfare, *Calle San Miguel*, is pedestrianised, the place for seeing and being seen. The range of leather bags, fashion jewellery, sunglasses and clothing is overwhelming.

## SIGHTSEEING

### JARDÍN BOTÁNICO MOLINO DE INCA
Clear spring water, fountains, palm trees and water features – an oasis outside the town to the north. Mills were operating here even in Moorish times. Today they are museum pieces and work with the push of a button. *Summer Tue–Sun 10am–2pm and 4pm–9pm, otherwise 10.30am–2pm and 4pm–6pm | Camino a los Manantiales*

### CASA DE LOS NAVAJAS
This is what holiday villas looked like around 100 years ago. The Neo-Mudéjar style in which a sugar baron had this luxurious mini palace built at the time is reminiscent of Alhambra. Now it's hidden away between blocks of high-rises off Playa del Bajondil. *Daily 11am–2pm, 6pm–8pm | entrance free*

## FOOD & DRINK

### CHIRINGUITO ISABEL
The mixed fish platter tastes even better with your toes in the sand. *Paseo Marítimo de la Carihuela 90 | tel. 95 237 20 33 | www.chiringuitoisabelellele.com | Budget–Moderate*

### BODEGA QUITAPENAS
Sit right at the heart of things, and enjoy a meal of fried fish, sardines, squid and Málaga sweet wine straight from the barrel. Has a terraced area. *Daily | Calle Cuesta del Tajo 3 | tel. 9 52 38 62 44 | Budget*

## BEACHES

Torremolinos' main asset is 7 km/4.5 mi of beaches with extensive sunbathing areas and good infrastructure. Over the years, the former beach bars *(chiringuitos)* have transformed themselves into fancy restaurants. *Playa de la Carihuela* stretches away to the southwest, towards Benalmádena, and the main beach, *Playa del Bajondillo,* points northeast.

## SPORTS & ACTIVITIES

The water park, *Aqualand (daily 11am–6pm, July/Aug until 7pm | www.aqualand.es)* and the *Crocodile Park* (see 'Travel with Kids' chapter) are both located in the northern part of Torremolinos.

## ENTERTAINMENT

A popular nightlife zone is *Playa de los Álamo.* A gay scene centres on clubs such as *Passion (Avenida de Mallorca 18 | www.passiondisco.com).* The crowds ebb and flow until late at night in and around Calle San Miguel.

## WHERE TO STAY

### HOSTAL GUADALUPE
Situated at the interface between town and beach and therefore not for those in search of peace and quiet. All rooms en suite. *14 rooms | Calle del Peligro 15 | tel. 9 52 38 19 37 | www.hostalguadalupe. com | Budget*

### MELIÁ COSTA DEL SOL
Double hotel block right on Playa del Bajondillo. The hotel has two restaurants, swimming pool and thalassotherapy centre. Attractive online rates. *538 rooms | Paseo Marítimo 11 | tel. 9 12 76 47 47 | www.hotelmeliacostadelsol.com | Moderate*

## INFORMATION

*Plaza de las Comunidades Autónomas | tel. 9 52 37 19 09 | www.torremolinos.es*

The rise of the Costa del Sol began on the beaches of Torremolinos in the 1960s

# COSTA DEL SOL AROUND MARBELLA

The stunning panoramas of beaches and mountains here are as natural as the Botox-enhanced smart set relaxing in the marina of Puerto Banús are artificial – in the western part of the Sun Coast, contrasts and clichés converge.

The region is renowned for its many miles of wide sandy beaches, which have helped to make cities like Estepona, Marbella and Fuengirola such appealing destinations. The flip side: in high season these very accessible beaches get completely packed. The busy A7 coast road and the parallel AP7 coastal motorway form a kind of boundary. If you're here on a beach holiday, you shouldn't stay any further north than that.

In the distant hinterland, you can reach the dreamy village of Casares and magi-

cal Ronda. For something completely different, you can take an excursion to Gibraltar – a little piece of Britain hanging off the southern tip of Andalusia.

# ESTEPONA

**(129 E4) (*M E6*) Estepona (pop. 67,000) began life back in the 16th century as a tiny settlement of 30 families. It has now developed into a fully-fledged holiday resort and yachting haven at the western end of the Costa del Sol.**

The modern tourism developments stand in sharp contrast to the attractive Old Town, with its lanes and chalk-white houses. Along the beach promenades fountains, bulbous street lamps, lawns

## Beach fun, marinas and promenades: everything from down-to-earth to chic on the coast and picture-postcard white villages inland

and palm trees reflect the taste of the modern planners. You can see a long way from Estepona – Gibraltar and Africa looming in the distance, and the Sierra Bermeja rearing up behind.

### SIGHTSEEING

#### PLAZA DE LAS FLORES

Orange trees, flowerbeds, fountains, cafés and benches make the 'Flower Square', the jewel of Estepona's Old Town. It isn't far from here to the church of *Nuestra*

*Señora de los Remedios* dating from the 18th century, and the *Plaza del Reloj* with its araucaria trees and bandstand. In the surrounding neighbourhood life goes on as normal.

#### PUERTO DEPORTIVO

A slender little lighthouse marks the presence of the large marina, which has almost 450 berths. Here the yachting fraternity and nightlife scene converge on bars, pubs and restaurants to suit every taste.

## FOOD & DRINK

### LA CASA DEL REY

The furnishings of this centrally located gastropub and vinoteca are modern, as are its interpretations of (tapas) recipes. Delicious tapas are served with the wine tasting on Thursday evenings *(25 euros | reservation tel. 6 08 91 79 94). Daily | Calle*

## BEACHES

The harbour moles jut out between the two long sections of well-kept beach – *Playa de la Rada* in the east and *Playa del Cristo* in the west. A few miles to the west of the town, everything is as nature intended at the nudist beach of *Costa Natura*.

Behind Estepona, Casares straddles the hillside in the Sierra Bermeja

*Raphael 7 | tel. 9 51 96 54 14 | lacasadel reyestepona.com | Moderate*

### LA ESCOLLERA

This simple restaurant on the fishing harbour is a must for all fish lovers. Very few frills, but the freshest seafood and almost exclusively locals. Get there early, it fills up quite quickly. *Closed Sun evening and Mon | Prto. Pesquero| tel. 9 52 80 63 54| facebook: La Escollera Estepona | Budget*

## SPORTS & ACTIVITIES

Diving courses at *Happy Diver's Club (Atalaya Park Hotel | Ctra. de Cádiz km 168.5 | tel. 9 52 88 36 17 | www.happy-divers-marbella.com).*

## ENTERTAINMENT

### PEÑA FLAMENCA

Famous flamenco singers, dancers and guitar-players perform here at the Gala

Flamenca every Friday from 9.30pm. Tapas and drinks are also served next to the stage. It's a good idea to reserve a table, just in case. *Calle Fuerzas Armadas | tel. 9 52 80 31 83*

### KEMPINSKI HOTEL
### BAHÍA ESTEPONA
One of several 5-star hotels in and around Estepona, the Kempinski leaves nothing to be desired. It has a lovely garden, large landscaped pool area and superb restaurants. *133 rooms | Ctra. de Cádiz km 159 | Playa El Padrón | tel. 9 52 80 95 00 | www.kempinski.com | Expensive*

### HOSTAL LA MALAGUEÑA
In the Old Town, just a stone's throw from Plaza de las Flores. Inexpensive and simply furnished, but all rooms are en suite. *16 rooms | Calle Raphael 1 | tel. 9 52 80 00 11 | www.hlmestepona.com | Budget*

## INFORMATION

*Plaza de las Flores | tel. 9 52 80 20 02 | www.estepona.es*

## WHERE TO GO

### BENAHAVÍS (129 E4) (*ⓜ E6*)
Reached through eucalyptus groves and the gorge of the Río Guadalmina, this village is known as the 'dining room of Costa del Sol'. Here the cuisine is specialised, in particularly, in stews with game, lamb, partridge, suckling pig or rabbit. Every other house seems to be a restaurant here in the warren of alleys in this classic white village, where two-thirds of the 8000 inhabitants are foreigners, with no shortage of millionaires among them. Those hungry for meat are sure to rub their bellies in satisfaction at the rustic *Los Abanicos (closed Tue | Calle Málaga 15 | tel. 9 52 85 50 22 | Moderate).* Those in need of some movement after the generous portions should go for a hike through the green mountains all around. Sport is certainly in here: *Gran Hotel Benahavís* often serves as a training camp for top international football clubs or national teams.

### CASARES ★ ●
(129 E4) (*ⓜ D6*)
The ⬈ winding road towards Casares (pop. 5700), 20 km/13 mi to the west of Estepona, affords glimpses of this moun-

★ **Casares**
Picturesque white village in the Estepona hinterland → **p. 83**

★ **Upper Rock Nature Reserve**
Join the wild Barbary apes on the Rock of Gibraltar → **p. 84**

★ **Teleférico Benalmádena**
Take the cable car up Monte Calamorro for a view of Africa → **p. 87**

★ **Puerto Deportivo in Benalmádena**
Colourful goings-on around the marina → **p. 86**

★ **Plaza de los Naranjos in Marbella**
Idyllic place to convene beneath the orange trees → **p. 88**

★ **Tajo Gorge in Ronda**
The gorge of the Río Guadalevín creates a spectacular cleft in one of Spain's most beautiful towns → **p. 91**

tain village high above. Then, as you round the bend, it appears at close quarters: a sea of white houses. At the centre of the village is the Plaza de España with its fountain, *La Bodeguita de en Medio* restaurant *(daily | Plaza España 15 | tel. 9 52 89 40 36 | Budget–Moderate)* and a

Spanish or British? Some of Gibraltar's inhabitants don't really care

couple of bars. Above the square, alleys lead up to the church and the ᴺᴸ castle ruins, from where there are magnificent views of the mountainous surroundings. Despite the influx of visitors, Casares manages to retain an almost unspoilt village atmosphere. Clothes are aired in front of the houses, flowerpots hang on the window grills, and in the evening the smell of food and the sound of TV waft through the alleyways. *www.casares.es*

## GIBRALTAR
## (129 D5) *(ᴍ D7)*

A limestone massif, 425 m/1394 ft high, called The Rock for short, Gibraltar (pop. 30,000) is a little bit of Britain at the southern tip of Andalusia. In 1704, the English stormed the rock, and much to the chagrin of Spain have never handed it back. This small political hot potato has *fish 'n' chips,* Royal Mail letterboxes and an approach road that curiously cuts right across the airport runway.

Gibraltar, which lies 50 km/31 mi southwest of Estepona, is worth a day trip, but watch out: British-Spanish disagreements have intensified in recent times, as has harassment by Spanish border guards. Car parks are few and far between, so it's best to leave your car in La Línea de la Concepción (charged parking) and cross the border on foot. On the other side, buses and taxis run to spots such as ᴺᴸ *Europa Point* at the southern end of the town, from where there are great views of the shipping in the Straits of Gibraltar and across to Morocco's Rif Mountains, their outline just discernible in the distance.

And then it's up in the cable car to the ★ ᴺᴸ *Upper Rock Nature Reserve;* a combined ticket including cable car entitles you to visit the small *St Michael's Cave,* the *Great Siege Tunnels,* which were dug into the Rock during the Spanish-French siege of 1779– 83, and the *Moorish Castle (combined ticket 29 pounds, children (aged 5–12) 17.50 pounds | daily 9.30am–5.15pm, March–Oct until 7.15pm | gibraltarinfo.gi).* Along the way, you'll encounter Barbary apes, which delight in cavorting around on car roofs, defecating and then pouncing on anything that looks like it might be food. Actually feeding the apes is strictly forbidden, on pain of a heavy fine! It's also possible to drive up by taxi or in your own car; there are more great views of the Gulf of Algeciras below.

The town's main shopping thoroughfare is *Main Street*, where many shops *(closed Sat pm and Sun)* sell alcohol, electronic goods, perfume and jewellery.

# FUENGIROLA

**(130 B6)** *(Ⓜ F6)* **Another mega holiday centre on the Costa del Sol, fully dedicated to tourism with its 8-km-/ 5-mi-long, 40-m-wide sand beaches. The great leisure opportunities attract hordes of holiday-hungry tourists to the 75,000-person town every year.**

Popular places to go include the large marina and Plaza de la Constitución. Walkers, joggers and cyclists share the beach promenade *(Paseo Marítimo)*, which crosses the Río Fuengirola via a modern bridge on the south side of town. Playgrounds in the sand underline the family-friendliness of the beaches.

## SIGHTSEEING

### CASTILLO SOHAIL

The rebuilt castle, which originally dates from medieval times, is perched on a green hill above the southern Ejido beach. The walls and towers serve as the setting for various events during the summer, ranging from concerts to the *Mercado Medieval. Tue–Sun 10am– 2pm, Sat/Sun also 3.30pm–6pm (in summer 6.30pm–9.30pm | entrance free | Calle Tartesos*

## FOOD & DRINK

### AROMA

Mediterranean cuisine with fresh fish and meats, including some exotically spiced dishes. If it's too full here, there are plenty of alternatives on the same street. *Closed Tue | Calle Moncayo 23 | tel. 9 52 66 55 02 | facebook: Restaurante Aroma Fuengirola | Moderate*

### EL HIGUERÓN

Situated some 7 km/4 ml to the north of Fuengirola, this is a classic among the Costa del Sol's restaurants. Andalusian cuisine (especially fish) is represented, as are dishes from northern Spain such as *fabada* (Asturian bean stew). *Daily | Ctra. Benalmádena–Mijas km 3.1 | tel. 9 52 11 91 63 | www.elhigueron.com | Expensive*

### VEGETALIA

Vegetarian eatery serving up a huge range of dishes, from soya balls to curried rice and stuffed peppers for 9.50 euros. *Closed Sun and evenings | Calle Santa Isabel 8 | near the Los Boliches train station | tel. 9 52 58 60 31 | restaurantevegetalia. com | Budget*

## SPORTS & ACTIVITIES

There are boat tours from the marina, as well as diving excursions with *Abysub (tel. 6 57 64 49 06 | www.abysub.com)*. In the centre there's a zoo *(daily 10am–at least 6pm, in summer occasionally until 11pm | 20.50 euros, children (aged 3–9) 15.50 euros, online discounts | Calle Camilo José Cela 6–8 | www.bioparcfuen girola.es)*.

The *Aquapark (mid-April–mid-Sept daily 10am–at least 5.30pm, in summer occasionally until 7pm | 26.50 euros, children (aged 8–12) 20.50 euros, (aged 3–7) 15.50 euros, discounts online | A 7 km 209 | www.aquamijas.com)* in Mijas-Costa is easy to get to. *Rancho La Paz* offers riding lessons and excursions, with an emphasis on animal welfare and the Iberian riding style.

## ENTERTAINMENT

The marina is where it's at – at least in high season! There are themed parties and live music in the *Boss (opposite Hotel Las Palmeras | facebook: Boss Disco Fuengirola)*. Spaniards are more likely to be found swarming around the Plaza de la Constitución.

## WHERE TO STAY

### MYRAMAR FUENGIROLA
Block with 224 well-equipped apartments (one or two bedrooms) at the far end of town. Popular choice with families with children. *Calle San Miguel 1 | tel. 9 52 58 87 68 | www.myramarhoteles.com | Moderate*

# LOW BUDGET

You can experience ● flamenco for free every Wednesday from noon on the *Plaza Virgen de la Peña* in *Mijas* – provided it's not raining or stormy.

There's a season ticket *(pase de temporada)* for *Selwo Aventura* (see the 'Travel with Kids' chapter), the marine park of *Selwo Marina* and the *cable car from Benalmádena* which allows an unlimited number of visits.

Marbella is pricey, but you can get an inexpensive night's sleep at the Youth Hostel *Albergue Inturjoven Marbella (Calle Trapiche 2 | tel. 9 55 18 11 81 | www.inturjoven.com)* in one of the 210 beds spread across 69 rooms. There's even a pool in summer.

### LAS RAMPAS
A good 3-star hotel with restaurant and a small pool. The beaches are within easy walking distance. *159 rooms | Calle Pintor Nogales | tel. 9 52 47 09 00 | www.hotellasrampas.com | Budget–Moderate*

## INFORMATION

*Paseo Jesús Santos Rein 6 | tel. 9 52 46 74 57 | www.visitafuengirola.com*

## WHERE TO GO

### BENALMÁDENA
**(130 B6) (⌘ F6)**
Benalmádena (pop. 68,000) is around 10 km/6 mi northeast of Fuengirola, spread out among the far-flung districts of *Benalmádena Pueblo, Arroyo de la Miel* and *Benalmádena Costa*. It is heavily developed and hopelessly confusing but also has 9 km/5.5 mi of beaches, elegant promenades and plenty of recreational facilities. Benalmádena combines an unusual mix of attractions: a modern 33-m-/108-ft-high Buddhist temple *Estupa de la Iluminación (Tue–Sat 10am–2pm and 4pm–7pm | entrance free | El Retamar | www.stupabenalmadena.org)*, the nearby *Mariposario* butterfly house (see 'Travel with Kids' chapter), the neo-Arabic *Castillo del Bil-Bil* (concerts, exhibitions) and right at the heart of the community the *Torrequebrada Golf Course (tel. 9 52 44 27 41 | www.golftorrequebrada.com)*

The focal point for the town's social scene is the ★ *Puerto Deportivo*. With more than 1000 berths, it is one of the largest and most attractive marinas on Spain's Mediterranean coast. The whole place looks very artificial with building complexes in neo-Moorish style, but it has a lot to offer visitors. You can stroll around the yacht basins and jetties and

Even a run-of-the-mill resort like Benalmádena has quiet corners: façade in the Pueblo district

there's a great choice of shops, restaurants, pubs and cafés. There are boat trips around the harbour, boat services to Málaga and Fuengirola, sailing, little bridges strung with lanterns, boutiques, expensive ice cream parlours, sangria by the litre, disco rhythms and the *Sealife Aquarium (daily 10am–7.30pm | 16 euros, children (aged 3–9) 13.50 euros, discounts online | www.visitsealife.com).*
The *Parque de la Paloma,* with its paths and ponds, is situated a short way inland. Next to that is the not exactly cheap marine park of *Selwo Marina (staggered opening times, see website | selwomarina.es).* The highlights here are the dolphin and sea lion shows, but there are also penguins, pelicans, flamingos, iguanas and caimans.
In the Arroyo de la Miel district there is a theme park, *Tivoli World (staggered opening times, see website | www.tivoli.es)* with a range of rides and amusements. Right next to it is the start of one of the best cable car rides in the country – the

3-km-/1.8-mi-long ★ ● *Teleférico Benalmádena (staggered opening times, see website | telefericobenalmadena.com).* It takes just 15 minutes to get to the top of the 769-m/2523-ft Monte Calamorro, where paths lead off to various view points. The coast lies spread out below, and in the distance you can see the outline of Africa. Impressive! Note, however, that in strong winds the cable car may not operate. The ticket price includes a falconry display *(exhibición de aves rapaces, daily 1pm),* during which you can observe bald eagles and griffon vultures circling above the mountain range.

### MIJAS (130 B6) (*Ɯ F6*)
The dazzling white of the houses, the neat alleyways and original architecture make this hillside village (pop. 5500) 8 km/5 mi to the north of Fuengirola in the Sierra de Mijas an attractive destination for an excursion. Buses from the resorts ensure a stress-free journey. There are superb views of the coastal plain both

from the 🌿 garden next to the ruined Moorish castle in the upper village and the 🌿 viewing terrace next to the *Santuario de la Virgen de la Peña*. This sanctuary has been carved out of the rock and contains an image of the Virgin.

It's worth looking at the exhibition of Picasso ceramics at the contemporary art centre *CAC (Tue–Sun 10am–7pm | 3 euros | Calle Málaga 28 | www.cacmijas.info)*. Also stages changing exhibitions. The small *bullring* is every bit as welcoming to visitors as the museum of miniatures, the *Carromato de Mijas (daily 10am–6pm, Easter–June 10am–8pm, July–Oct 10am–10pm | 3 euros, children (aged 6–14) 1.50 euros | Avda. del Compás)*. But the 'donkey taxis' should be boycotted – this is purely cruelty to animals.

# MARBELLA

(129 F4) *(ﾛ E6)* **This overgrown beach town (pop. 141,000) still cultivates its reputation as an exclusive resort and celebrity haven.**

Always that bit smarter and posher than elsewhere, whether it's the classy restaurants, the oversized conference centre, palm trees set in marble planters or the numerous golf courses nearby. The

> **CITY WHERE TO START?**
> **Plaza de los Naranjos**, 'Orange Tree Square', is the best place to soak up Marbella's Old Town atmosphere. The bus station is just outside town on Avenida del Trapiche; from there take bus L3 into the centre. Centrally located car parks include Parking Avenida del Mar, Parking de la Constitución and Parking Edificio Parquesol.

flipside of all this is a series of corruption scandals, which has earned the city some negative international publicity. In the Old Town around the Plaza de los Naranjos, however, Marbella shows itself from its more attractive, evocative side.

## SIGHTSEEING

### OLD TOWN
A criss-cross of alleyways, a few remnants of the old town wall and the ⭐ *Plaza de los Naranjos* comprise Marbella's Old Town. The square is a beautiful, colourful place with cafés and restaurants, and, of course, the eponymous orange trees. In the middle of the square there's a bust of the Spanish king Juan Carlos I, and pigeons cool off in a fountain. In the southeast corner is the diminutive Ermita de Santiago, the town's oldest religious building, dating from the 15th century. It is the headquarters of the *Santo Cristo del Amor religious brotherhood*. Much larger is the nearby *Iglesia de Nuestra Señora de la Encarnación*, a cool escape during hot weather.

### AVENIDA DEL MAR
Along this pedestrianised section of road, branching off the beach promenade, you can admire the little **INSIDER TIP** *open-air gallery*, which has sculptures by Salvador Dalí. Works include 'Man on Dolphin', 'Don Quixote Seated', 'Cosmic Elephant' and 'Gala at the Window' featuring Dalí's wife and muse. A fountain and flowerbeds enhance the mini sculpture park.

### MUSEO RALLI
This museum of modern art on the coast road towards Puerto Banús has chosen surrealism and magic realism as its focus. The collection of South American art, including work by Wilfredo Lam and Alicia Carletti is particularly impressive. *Tue–Sat 10am–3pm | entrance free |*

Marbella's Plaza de los Naranjos is particularly captivating in the evening

*Urbanización Coral Beach, N-340 km 176 |*
*museoralli.es*

### MUSEO DEL GRABADO ESPAÑOL CONTEMPORÁNEO

The art museum housed in the Renaissance Hospital de Bazán has temporary exhibitions of prints by contemporary famous artists. *Mon, Sat 9am–2pm, Tue–Fri 9am–7pm | entrance free | Calle Hospital de Bazán | mgec.es*

### PARQUE DE LA CONSTITUCIÓN

Small municipal park near the beach promenade, with cypresses, palm trees, banana plants and bamboo stands. It has a pleasant INSIDER TIP *park café*, where many locals meet.

## FOOD & DRINK

### ALTAMIRANO

Typically Spanish with loyal local clientele. Ultra-fresh seafood only. *Closed Wed | Plaza Altamirano 3 | tel. 9 52 82 49 32 |* *facebook: Bur Altamirano Marbella | Budget–Moderate*

### BIBO

Exquisite fusion cooking without having to mortgage your house. In star chef Dani García's gourmet bistro the atmosphere is pleasantly casual. *Hotel Puente Romano, Av. Bulevar Príncipe Alfonso de Hohenlohe | tel. 9 52 76 42 52 | www.grupo danigarcia.com | Moderate–Expensive*

### D.O.MAR

In this new restaurant at the heart of the golden mile (formerly Les Cubes), the sea view and tasteful furnishings also provide a feast for the eyes. *Closed Mon | N340 km 183 | Urbanización Oasis Club | tel. 9 52 86 83 96 | domarmarbella.com | Expensive*

## SHOPPING

Marbella lives up to its reputation as an exclusive shopping location *(www.*

shopping-marbella.com). There's a good choice of boutiques, especially along *Avenida Ricardo Soriano*. The largest shopping centre is *Centro Comercial La Cañada* on the road to Ojén. Puerto Banús is an option for those with the right budget.

## BEACHES

The marina *La Bajadilla* separates the beaches within the town area. Parallel to the western beaches runs the *Paseo Marítimo*, a strolling promenade, which is also used by cyclists and inline-skaters.

## SPORTS & ACTIVITIES

Waterskiing, jet-skiing, parasailing, flyboarding – *Aquatime at Playa Hotel Marbella Club (Bulevar Principe Alfonso | tel. 6 86 48 80 68 | aquatimemarbella.com) offers a whole range of water sports fun*. You can book a diving course at *(tel. 6 11 27 15 21 | buceaenmarbella.com)*. There are several internationally renowned golf courses in the surrounding area.

## ENTERTAINMENT

A pleasant old-town atmosphere pervades the *Plaza de los Naranjos.* The marina is a popular place to meet up for cocktails. The long-standing star of Marbella's nightlife is the oriental-style, very exclusive *Olivia Valère nightclub (Ctra. de Istán km 0.8 | www.oliviavalere.com)*.

## WHERE TO STAY

### CASA LA CONCHA

A stylish boutique hotel, off the beaten track. Book early, as there are only four suites and six cottages! *Calle Jubrique 45 | Urbanización Rocío de Nagüeles | tel. 6 46 52 08 83 | www.casalaconcha. com | Expensive*

### LA MORADA MÁS HERMOSA

Small and friendly and in the heart of the Old Town. Some rooms have a balcony or small roof terrace. Rooms are well equipped and provide good value for money. *7 rooms | Calle Montenebros 16 a | tel. 9 52 92 44 67 | www.lamoradamas hermosa.com | Moderate*

## INFORMATION

*Glorieta de la Fontanilla | tel. 9 52 77 14 42 | www.marbellaexclusive.com*

## WHERE TO GO

### PUERTO BANÚS ●
### (129 F4) (𝖔 E6)

Smart, smarter, Puerto Banús. In Marbella's neighbour 5 km/3 mi to the southwest (boat services from and to Marbella marina), people like showing off what they have. The marina is one long catwalk, on which celebrities regularly appear, sporting killer heels, status handbags, little white dogs and tons of jewellery, not to mention Botox and silicone. Sometimes reality beats the clichées. The marina is the perfect place to observe this fascinating spectacle, but it's also nice for an evening out. All around the harbour basin are restaurants, cocktail bars and boutiques, generally catering to a very wealthy clientele. The 1-km-/0.6-mi-long beach stretches east of the town, in the direction of Marbella. Behind the marina, there's more going on at *Plaza Antonio Banderas.*

### RONDA (129 E3) (𝖔 E5)

A visit to Ronda, situated around 60 km/37 mi northwest of Marbella, is one of the highlights of a trip to Andalusia. Even the journey there along the A397 through the mountains of the Serranía de Ronda is an experience. The town (pop. 37,000) is perilously perched on a clifftop and divided by the more than 100-m/330-ft deep ★ *Tajo Gorge*. It is impressively spanned by the Puente Nuevo (New Bridge); at the bottom flows the Río Guadalevín.

'La Mina' is a INSIDERTIP secret passage with more than 230 steep steps through

cent | *colegiataronda.com)*, built over the former mosque, the historic *Palacio de Mondragón* with local museum *(Mon–Fri 10am–6pm, in summer until 7pm, Sat/Sun 10am–3pm | 3.50 euros, free for EU citizens Tue from 3pm | Plaza Mondragón | www.turismoderonda.es)*, the Arab Baths *(Baños Árabes | Mon–Fri 10am–*

There's no point watching the pennies on your tour of the boutiques at Puerto Banús marina

the rock that leads down to *Mina de Agua* on the river *(daily 10am–8pm | Mai–Sept until 9.30pm | 5 euros | Calle Cuesta de Santo Domingo 9 | casadelreymoro.org with a link to a free audio guide in English)*. The Moors created the tunnel in the 14th century as a means of protecting the water supply in the event of a siege.

There's plenty to discover in Ronda, from the alleyways of the Old Town, the church of *Santa María la Mayor (daily 10am–6pm/7pm/8pm | 4.50 euro incl. English audio guide | Plaza de la duquesa de Par-*

6pm/7pm, Sat/Sun 10am–3pm | 3.50 euros, free Tue from 3pm)* and the *Bullfighting Arena* dating from 1785 *(daily 10am–6pm/7pm, in summer until 8pm | 7 euros, Mon 8am–10am, Tue/Wed 9am–10am free for EU citizens | Calle Virgen de la Paz 15)*.

A stroll across the Plaza de España and through the pedestrianised area around Carrera Espinel, as well as a walk in the small municipal park of *Alameda del Tajo* (the ☼ terrace with views of the Sierra de Grazalema is a real treat), round off a visit to the town.

# DISCOVERY TOURS

## **1** **THE COSTA DEL SOL AT A GLANCE**

**START:** **1** Málaga
**END:** **1** Málaga

**12 days**
Actual driving time
approx. 18–24 hours

Distance:
🚗 approx. 900 km/560 mi

**COSTS:** approx. 1800–2000 euros/2 people (fuel, accommodation, admission fees, food)

**IMPORTANT TIPS:** Book your Alhambra visit (early!) and hotels in **9** Granada in advance!

Drink a cocktail on the 'Balcony of Europe', immerse yourself in the desert landscape of Almería, wander in the footsteps of the Moors in white-painted villages and on a visit to the Alhambra in Granada, let yourself be captivated by the mys-

Would you like to explore the places that are unique to this region? Then the Discovery Tours are just the thing for you – they include terrific tips for stops worth making, breathtaking places to visit, selected restaurants and fun activities. It's even easier with the Touring App: download the tour with map and route to your smartphone using the QR Code on pages 2/3 or from the website address in the footer below – and you'll never get lost again even when you're offline.

**TOURING APP**

→ p. 2/3

tic mountain world around Ronda, savour the exquisite tapas in Málaga's Old Town and some grilled fish in one of the beach restaurants: experience the many facets of the Costa del Sol!

Start your tour at a car-hire agency at the airport in **❶ Málaga** → p. 64 – there are plenty of them. For your first taste of the coast, head for **❷ Nerja** → p. 74, **just under an hour to the east.** The place where everyone gets together is the expansive esplanade, the **Balcón de Europa**. At sunset, the beach bars are an inviting place for a

**DAY 1**

**❶ Málaga**

(54 km/33.5 mi)

**❷ Nerja**

🌿 🍸 🎵 🚗

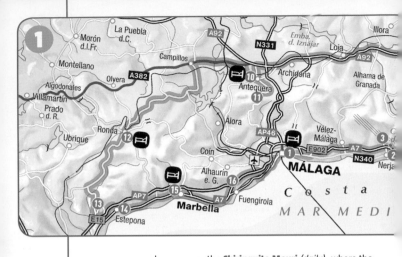

sundower, e. g. the **Chiringuito Mauri** *(daily),* where the grilled sardines taste particularly good.

**DAY 2**

13 km/8 mi

**❸ Frigiliana**

27 km/17 mi

**❹ Almuñécar**

**Continue inland for a few miles on the minor road MA-5105** to picturesque **❸ Frigiliana** → p. 77. Over a few delicious French-style tapas and a glass of wine, enjoy the magnificent view from the terrace of the **INSIDER TIP La Esquina del Bandolero** *(daily | Calle El Portón 2 | tel. 6 94 50 14 18 | Budget).* **Leave the mountains and return to the coast, heading towards Motril. After roughly half an hour you reach ❹ Almuñécar** → p. 45. It's worth staying overnight in the main town on the Costa Tropical, since you can take a boat trip to watch the dolphins and whales off the coast at Almuñécar. **Sailnplay** in La Herradura *(sailnplay.com)* offers catamaran tours.

**DAY 3–4**

151 km/94 mi

**❺ Almería**

48 km/30 mi

**❻ San José**

**DAY 5–7**

69 km/43 mi

**❼ Desierto de Tabernas**

73 km/45 mi

**The route continues eastwards,** in some places leading you through a glittering, almost surreal plastic world of greenhouses. The fabulous fortress in **❺ Almería** → p. 32 is a tempting stop on the way, before the journey continues into the **Cabo de Gata Nature Reserve**. Ideally, you should stay for two nights in **❻ San José** → p. 41. The following day is beach day: crystal-clear water off the **beaches** to the southwest of San José are perfect for bathing, snorkelling and diving against the wild, romantic coastal backdrop!

**Say goodbye, at least for a while, to the sea and head through the semi-desert, the ❼ Desierto de Tabernas**

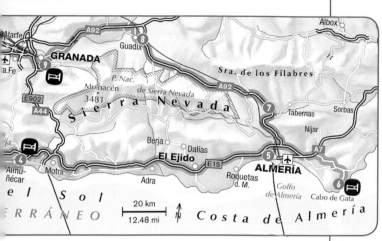

→ p. 37, **towards ⑧ Guadix** → p. 62, where a curious form of habitation – underground caves – is worth a closer look. **The A 92 leads over the 1380-m/4527-ft high pass, Puerto de la Mora, on to ⑨ Granada** → p. 48. Stay here for three nights to give yourself enough time for the legendary Moorish palace, the **Alhambra**, for some tapas tours, a stroll through the Old Town, the **Capilla Real**, the **cathedral** and the labyrinthine district of **Albaicín**.

**To the west of Granada, the motorway takes you to ⑩ Antequera** → p. 71, from where you set off on a roughly two-hour hike through the **⑪ El Torcal de Antequera Nature Reserve to the south of the town**. At the end of your hike, be sure to go the few extra steps to the viewpoint, **Mirador las Ventanillas** – it's well worth it!

**Continuing southwestwards, you finally reach ⑫ Ronda** → p. 90, another typically enchanting Andalusian destination. The small town is literally bisected by the **Tajo Gorge**, formed over thousands of years by the Río Guadalevín eating away through the rock.

**Leaving the mountain landscape behind, the winding road cuts down through white-painted villages clinging to the hillsides, such as ⑬ Casares** → p. 83 (fine views from the **ruined castle!**), **to the western Costa del Sol.** Here, stop at one of the long **beaches** at **⑭ Estepona** → p. 80 for a swim, a few tapas and a refreshing drink.

⑧ Guadix

*54 km/33.5 mi*

⑨ Granada

**DAY 8**

*111 km/69 mi*

⑩ Antequera

*15 km/9 mi*

⑪ El Torcal de Antequera Nature Reserve

**DAY 9**

*103 km/64 mi*

⑫ Ronda

**DAY 10**

*55 km/34 mi*

⑬ Casares

*27 km/17 mi*

⑭ Estepona

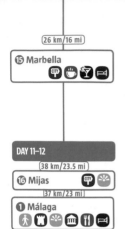

**15** Marbella

26 km/16 mi

Maybe you'll be lucky and catch the smell of *espetos* (sardine kebabs) being grilled in front of one of the *chiringuitos*! **The next stage of your trip is the legendary town of 15 Marbella → p. 88.** Don't be put off by the sprawling suburbs of this jet-set destination; visit the attractive Old Town and be sure to stay overnight there. An aperitif or an ice-cream on the almost-too-pretty-to-be-true **Plaza de los Naranjos**: that does have quite considerable charm, despite the hordes of tourists!

**DAY 11–12**

38 km/23.5 mi

**16** Mijas

37 km/23 mi

**1** Málaga

Gradually, the route begins to turn back and passes the holiday hotspots Fuengirola and Torremolinos. Don't miss a final detour to the much-visited **16 Mijas → p. 87** high above the coast. Treat yourself to a whole day in **1 Málaga**. Take a walk up to the **Castillo de Gibralfaro** with a 360-degree view over the towns and cities of the Costa del Sol. Visit the **Picasso Museum** and the **Centre Pompidou** at the harbour, stopping every now and then for some tapas in the bustling **Old Town**.

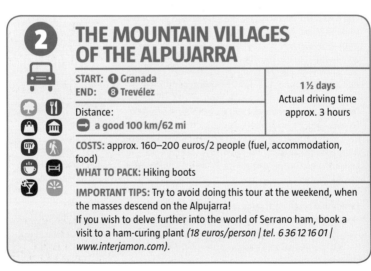

## 2

# THE MOUNTAIN VILLAGES OF THE ALPUJARRA

**START: 1 Granada**
**END: 8 Trevélez**

**1 ½ days**
Actual driving time
approx. 3 hours

**Distance:**
→ a good 100 km/62 mi

**COSTS:** approx. 160–200 euros/2 people (fuel, accommodation, food)

**WHAT TO PACK:** Hiking boots

**IMPORTANT TIPS:** Try to avoid doing this tour at the weekend, when the masses descend on the Alpujarra!

If you wish to delve further into the world of Serrano ham, book a visit to a ham-curing plant *(18 euros/person | tel. 6 36 12 16 01 | www.interjamon.com)*.

Gorges, green river valleys, stacks of whitewashed houses arranged on the hillsides like a work of art: the ★ **La Alpujarra** mountain range is one of the most attractive regions in Andalusia. Squeezed in between the southern foothills of the Sierra Nevada and the coastal mountains, it leaves visitors breathless. After the fall of Granada in 1492, many expelled Moors took refuge there, leaving a legacy of ruined fortresses, terraced agriculture and sophisticated irrigation systems

The first stage of the journey from **❶ Granada → p. 48** is an unspectacular drive **on the A 44 as far as the La Alpujarra/Lanjarón exit.** But on the **minor road A 348** you'll soon be captivated by the mountain world in which olives, oranges and almonds flourish. Stop briefly **at the entrance** to the spa resort of **❷ Lanjarón**: the **tourist information office** *(closed Mon | Av. de Madrid | tel. 9 58 77 04 62 | turismo.lanjanet.es)* has some helpful brochures. Lanjarón, the 'Gateway to the Alpujarra', is known for its therapeutic mineral waters, but you'll also find a host of souvenirs, such as pottery, basketware, honey, dried figs and pastries on sale too.

**The village is strung out along the hill, and beyond it the road winds its way onwards,** past olive groves, agaves, fig and pomegranate trees. **Shortly before reaching Órgiva, the route turns left onto the road to ❸ Pampaneira.** With its narrow alleys, white façades, trickling fountains, colourful tile decorations and burgeoning potted plants by the doorways, it is one of the prettiest villages in the entire province of Granada. In her **workshop** *(www.artesanos alpujarra.com)* **in Calle Águila,** Mercedes Carrascosa will show you how the rag rugs for which the village is famous are woven. Pop into the souvenir shop (with integrated bar), **Bodega La Moralea** *(Calle Verónica 4),* to stock up

**DAY 1**

**❶ Granada**

44 km/27 mi

**❷ Lanjarón**

23 km/14 mi

**❸ Pampaneira**

Alpujarra villages like Capileira are dotted across the southern foothills of the Sierra Nevada

5 km/3 mi

**④ Bubión** 🏛
2 km/1.2 mi

**⑤ Capileira** 🧗

5 km/3 mi

**⑥ La Cebadilla**

3 km/1.8 mi

**⑦ Capileira** 🍴 🛏

on some locally produced cheese and olive oil. For lunch, you are best advised to **leave the hustle and bustle of the main square in front of the church behind you** and head for **Casa Julio** *(closed Tue, except in Aug | Av. de la Alpujarra 9 | tel. 9 58 76 33 22 | www.casa-julio.com | Budget)* for some honest-to-goodness mountain fare.

**Beyond Pampaneira a detour leads via the elongated village of ④ Bubión** (note the artistic chimneys!) and up to **⑤ Capileira** sitting at an altitude of 1420 m/4658 ft. **In Castillo, the upper part of the village, set off on the hiking trail PR-A 69** on a 8-km/5-mi circuit. Even though it's only a relatively short distance, you should allow yourself around three and a half hours. It takes you through the gorge of the Río Poqueira along the base of the Mulhacén. **Initially, the path leads in the direction of the hydroelectric power station, the Central Hidroeléctrica del Poqueira. After around an hour you reach the deserted village of ⑥ La Cebadilla at 1540 m/5052 ft. A bridge takes you across the river; to the right, a narrow path heads back towards Capileira. You now cross the Puente de Abuchite bridge; walk uphill for roughly 1 km/0.6 mi and end up back in the village again. In ⑦ Capileira** you'll also find your bed for the night, e. g. at the **Hotel Rural Finca Los Llanos** *(40 rooms | tel. 9 58 76 30 71 | hotelfincaloslllanos. com | Budget–Moderate)*; the attached **restaurant** is open daily and serves specialities of the Alpujarra.

Back on the main road, attractive little villages continue to dot the route towards Trevélez: **first Pitres, then Pórtugos; between the two the road crosses the Río Bermejo.** At an altitude of almost 1500 m/4900 ft, you finally arrive at **❽ Trevélez**, its white houses clinging to the mountain slopes. Trevélez is famous for not just one, but two reasons: firstly, it is Spain's highest village – as announced by the colourful tiled sign at the entrance – and secondly, for the production of INSIDER TIP air-dried ham, known among connoisseurs as Serrano ham. Most of the retail outlets are **in the lower village,** where the aroma of the ham wafting onto the street is temptation enough to buy some. Bring your Alpujarra tour to a fitting close by trying some of the air-dried ham at the restaurant **La Fragua** *(daily | Calle Posadas | tel. 9 58 85 86 26 | www.hotellafragua.com | Budget–Moderate)*, with a sensational view of the rolling landscape of the Alpujarra thrown in!

**DAY 2**

24 km/15 mi

❽ Trevélez

---

## ❸ ON TWO WHEELS THROUGH THE CABO DE GATA NATURE RESERVE

| START: ❶ San José | 1 day |
| END: ❶ San José | Actual cycling time |
| Distance: 48 km/30 mi | approx. 4 hours |

**COSTS:** approx. 80 euros/2 people (bike hire, food)
**WHAT TO PACK:** Repair kit, drinking water, provisions, swimming things, sunscreen

**IMPORTANT TIPS:** Bike hire, among other things, at **Deportes Media Luna** *(Calle del Puerto 7 | tel. 9 50 38 04 62 | medialunaventura.com)*
It can get extremely hot!
The paths in the abandoned gold mine in ❻ **Rodalquilar** are in poor condition and should be followed only with extreme care.

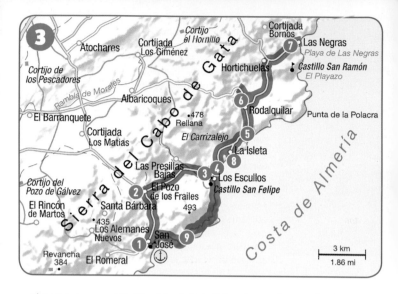

It's no longer a secret that the Cabo de Gata Nature Reserve is a paradise for nature lovers. Rather than gulping down clouds of dust on a bike tour southwestwards to the prettiest beaches and the cape, this excursion takes you in the opposite direction: with the wind in your face, you initially head inland. Get your energy levels back up on the quay at Las Negras harbour and with a swim in Isleta del Moro, before you set off on the last stage which takes you past prickly pears and agaves back to San José.

**1** San José

[ 3 km/1.8 mi ]

**2** El Pozo de los Frailes

[ 6 km/4 mi ]

**3** Los Escullos

[ 1 km/0.6 mi ]

**4** Playa del Arco

[ 5 km/3 mi ]

**5** Mirador
Las Amatistas

**10:00am** The tour kicks off with the short, roughly 3-km/ 1.8-mi stretch from **1** San José → p. 41 to the elongated village of **2** El Pozo de los Frailes, where a replica of a historic **waterwheel** *(noria)* has been built. **Just beyond El Pozo, take the road on the right to Los Escullos, Rodalquilar and Las Negras.** Thistles, prickly pears and agaves are the typical vegetation of the area.

The first turn-off leads you to **3** Los Escullos, where the sturdy fortress of **Castillo de San Felipe** seems a little out of place; it was built in the 18th century to guard against possible attacks from the sea. Close to the little settlement is **4** Playa del Arco, where you can plunge into the waters for a first cooling break. **Back on the main road, you pass the white coastal village of La Isleta del Moro on the right,** before arriving at the **5** Mirador Las Amatistas from where there are truly stunning panoramic views of the coast. **Once over the next shoulder**, the broad expanse of the Valle de Rodalquilar opens out below you. **You now embark on a precipitous descent (10 per cent gradient) – every mountain biker's dream!** In ❻ **Rodalquilar → p. 41**, the point on the tour that's furthest inland, you can visit the **abandoned gold mines in the upper village**. These conjure up memories of the former gold rush mentality in Rodalquilar. Some of the mines served as the backdrop to scenes from the film 'Indiana Jones and the Last Crusade'.

`01:00pm` The end of the road in ❼ **Las Negras marks the turning point of the tour.** Here, **on the quay at the harbour,** the traditional bar **La Bodeguyia** *(closed Mon/Tue | Calle Bahía de las Negras | Budget–Moderate)* **and, a few paces further on,** the **Las Barcas** *(daily | Calle Pescador 50 | restaurantelasbarcas.es | Budget–Moderate)* serve drinks and delicious tapas. ❽ **La Isleta del Moro → p. 41** is perfect for the next refreshing bathe on the way back – once you've got the tiring climb out of the Rodalquilar valley behind you.

`04:00pm` The return trip to San José takes you **from Los Escullos via the coastal track** – after all, you have hired a mountain bike! You pass the historic ❾ **watchtower** that is visible from ❶ **San José → p. 41**. Reward yourself with a cool drink at the bar **Monsul** *(closed Thu | Calle Correo 30)* just off the beach.

| 2 km/1.2 mi |
| ❻ Rodalquilar |
| 8 km/5 mi |
| ❼ Las Negras |
| 11 km/7 mi |
| ❽ La Isleta del Moro |
| 8 km/5 mi |
| ❾ Watchtower |
| 4 km/2.5 mi |
| ❶ San José |

Screaming 'water, here I come!', take the plunge under the eponymous arch at Playa del Arco

# 4

# MARBELLA SEA BREEZE AND SIERRA BLANCA MOUNTAIN AIR

**START:** ❶ Marbella
**END:** ❻ Ojén

**1 day**
Actual driving time
approx. 45 minutes

**Distance:**
🚗 a good 40 km/25 mi

**COSTS:** approx. 100 euros/2 people (fuel, food)
**WHAT TO PACK:** Swimming things, hiking boots, water

**IMPORTANT TIPS:** The hiking route is only sporadically signposted.

On a morning stroll along the beach promenade, breathe in the atmosphere of drop-dead chic Marbella. After that, set off for the barren mountains of the Sierra Blanca, which rise up into the sky behind the town.

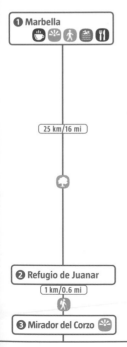

❶ Marbella
☕ 🏖 🚶 🌊 🍴

25 km/16 mi

🌳

❷ Refugio de Juanar
1 km/0.6 mi
🚶

❸ Mirador del Corzo 🏖

**10:00am** Following your breakfast with a view of the sea at the **Cappuccino** *(daily | in the Hotel Gran Meliá Don Pepe | Calle José Meliá | www.grupocappuccino.com)* in ❶ **Marbella → p. 88**, the **beach promenade** is perfect for a long walk **westwards on the wooden coastal walkway.** If you fancy, you can simply hop into the sea en route! On the way back, get your strength up again with a snack at **Garum** *(daily | tel. 9 52 85 88 58 | www.garummarbella. com | Moderate–Expensive)* **near the marina**.

**02:30pm** Leave the town on the N 340 towards Málaga and then follow the A 7 towards Algeciras as far as the exit marked A 355 for Ojén. Passing by Ojén, you drive on for around 10 km/6 mi, until you see the sign for 'El Refugio de Juanar'. You are now well and truly in the **Sierra Blanca**. It gets its name, 'white mountain range', from the pale rock and sparse vegetation. Chestnut and cherry trees as well as Spanish fir grow in the area, which is the habitat of the imperial eagle, deer and mountain goat. The air is heavy with the scent of pine trees, and the cicadas chirp as if their lives depended on it.

At the hotel ❷ **Refugio de Juanar** you begin your easy, three-hour hike on a circular route of a good 8 km/5 mi. **Initially, the road leads uphill as far as the observation point**, ❸ **Mirador del Corzo**. The town of Ojén lies be-

Away from the coast for a change: in the Sierra Blanca near the Refugio de Juanar

low you. Continue along the road, past the olive grove of Juanar, as far as the Puerto de Marbella pass. Now first orientate yourself towards Mirador del Macho Montés and then follow the zig-zag trail up to Puerto de la Viborilla. At the next fork in the path, ignore the one to Istán and follow the route in the direction of Llano de las Arenales. The path continues uphill as far as ④ **Puerto de Gurapalo**. Stop here for a moment to enjoy the fabulous panoramic view! **Now the path leads downhill until you reach the ⑤ Refugio de Juanar once again.**

**06:30pm** To round off your tour, it's a good idea to take a break in ⑥ **Ojén** first of all and take a look at the karst cave, **Cueva Alta**, which is open to the public. **The entrance is on the main road, Calle Carretera, and there's also an observation platform.** Afterwards, you can look forward to refreshments at the **Castillo Solis** *(closed Mon | Calle Ctra. | tel. 9 52 88 17 10 | Moderate)*. Settle down on the pleasant terrace and savour some typical local tapas, such as fried squid or mussels au gratin. It goes without saying that these should be accompanied by a digestif – a glass of **INSIDER TIP** locally distilled *aguardiente*.

6 km/4 mi

④ **Puerto de Gurapalo**

1 km/0.6 mi

⑤ **Refugio de Juanar**

11 km/7 mi

⑥ **Ojén**

# SPORTS & ACTIVITIES

Cycling and hiking, a round of golf, diving in crystal-clear water – every kind of sport and activity can be experienced on the Costa del Sol. And you'll even find free fitness apparatus on lots of the beaches and in many little villages, so there's no excuse not to work out.

## CLIMBING

The area around Caminito del Rey in Garganta del Chorro in the Málaga hinterland is very popular among climbing freaks from around the world. Other well-loved stomping grounds for escalada are *Cañón de Teba* (Málaga), *Cala del Moral* (Málaga), *Cogollos Vega* (Granada) and *Barranco de Cacín* near Fondón (Almería). You'll find a Spanish search engine for climbing schools at escuelasdeescalada.com.

## CYCLING & MOUNTAIN BIKING

Cycling is becoming ever more popular on the Costa del Sol and the number of bike paths and bike rentals is growing steadily. Cycling is particularly nice in the *Cabo de Gata Nature Reserve*, whereas the mountain region of Alpujarra provides much more strenuous terrain. In the summer the *Sierra Nevada Bike Park* (*sierranevadabikepark.com*) offers mountain bikers two lifts up to 8 different trails. Andalusia is well covered by cycling tour companies. *Andalucian Cycling Experience (tel. 9 52 18 40 42 | www.andaluciancyclingexperience.com)* operates from Montecorto in the Sierra de Grazalema west of Ronda and offers **INSIDER TIP** mountain biking holidays and road cycling

On land, on water or in the air: whatever you like doing, the coast and its hinterland provide plenty of activities all year round

trips as well as leisure cycling holidays and tough triathlon and winter training camps. *Biking Andalucia (tel. 6 76 00 25 46 / www. bikingandalucia.com)*, a British company based in Órgiva, specialises in mountain biking in the Sierra Nevada and Alpujarra; it offers a 7-day guided bike ride. By the way, in Spain the wearing of a helmet is compulsory for adult cyclists outside of cities, and everywhere for those under 16.

## DIVING

The best diving areas in this region are the Cabo de Gata Nature Reserve, the En- senada de las Entinas at Almerimar, the stretch between Castell de Ferro and Ca- lahonda, La Herradura near Almuñécar and the coast from Benalmádena Costa to Marbella.

The rocky coast of the Costa Tropical is a particularly popular base for diving schools, including *Buceo La Herradura (www.buceolaherradura.com)* at the Ma- rina del Este.

In the Cabo de Gata Nature Reserve, the *Isub (Calle Babor 3 | San José | www. isubsanjose.com)* diving centre offers courses and trips down into the crystal- clear underwater world.

## GOLF

Costa del Sol equals 'Costa del Golf': that's how the Sun Coast markets its many excellent golf courses. There are more than 60 courses spread across Málaga province alone. High season is spring and autumn; in summer, you'll find lots of special offers available. Spain's own golfing legend Severiano Ballesteros designed the course at ✏️ *Alhaurín Golf (A 387 Alhaurín el Grande–Mijas km 3.4 | www.alhauringolf.com)*, which has lovely views over the sea and the Sierra de Mijas. *Mijas Golf (Camino Viejo de Coín | Urbanización Mijas Golf | www.mijasgolf. org)* comprises the two 18-hole courses of Los Olivos and Los Lagos. Golfing and hotel packages are ideal for players from overseas. A luxury complex such as the *Villa Padierna Palace Hotel (Urbanización Los Flamingos Golf | villapadiernapalace hotel.com)* in the Marbella hinterland boasts a wide range of spa facilities as well as INSIDER TIP access to three 18-hole courses, located between Málaga and Torremolinos, the *Hotel Parador del Golf (www.golfenparadores.es)* offers an 18-hole course and a golf school. International rankings often classify the *Real Club de Golf Sotogrande (Paseo del Parque | Sotogrande | www.golfsotogrande.com)* among the best in Spain. Founded in 1964, the 18-hole course now rates as one of the most illustrious in Europe. The neighbouring *Club Valderrama (www.val derrama.com)* is almost as famous. Information on the courses and admission requirements can be found at *Federación Andaluza de Golf (tel. 9 52 22 55 90 | rfga. org)* and on the website *golfinspain.com*.

## HIKING

The mountainous Sierra Nevada, Sierras de Tejeda, Almijara y Alhama, Sierra de las Nieves and Alpujarra are popular walking areas, but don't expect the kind of signing you get in the Alps. Information is available from numerous websites such as *www.turgranada.es*, from local tourist offices in places like Lanjarón, in the visitor centres of the nature parks *(reservatu visita.es)* and from the *Federación Andaluza de Montañismo (www.fedamon.com)*. The Spanish National Geographic Institute online maps are very practical for orientation *(www.ign.es/iberpix2/visor)*. The Cabo de Gata Nature Reserve on the Almeria coast is a nice place to go walking. At *www.cabogataalmeria.com* click on *ocio y deporte > senderismo* to find diverse brochures on hiking trails which you can download for free; the descriptions are in Spanish, but the maps alone are sufficient help and give you some good ideas.

## HORSE RIDING

Riding schools offer one-to-one or group tuition as well as treks into the countryside. They include the *Escuela de Arte Equestre Costa del Sol (Calle Río Padrón Alto | escuela-ecuestre.com)* near Estepona, the *Centro Ecuestre Los Caireles (Camino de los Pescadores | Urbanización Hacienda Cortes | www.loscaireles.es)* near Marbella, or the *Club El Ranchito (Senda del Pilar 4 | ranchito.com)* near Torremolinos. Riding holidays lasting from a weekend to a week can be booked at *Cabacci (Alcudia de Guadix | Valle del Zalabi | www.cabacci.com)* in the province of Granada.

## PARAGLIDING

A popular spot for paragliding *(parapente)* is the *Valle de Abdalajís,* a valley to the southwest of Antequera in Málaga province. The following schools offer both tandem flights and courses lasting several days: *Eolox (www.para pentemalaga.es)* and *Líjar Sur (www. lijarsur.com)*.

## SKIING

Between November and March it's ski season in the Sierra Nevada. The ski resort of *Pradollano*, the southernmost in Europe, lies between 2100 m–2400 m/ 6900 ft–7900 ft and has 124 pistes on offer with a total length of 107 km/66 mi *(ski pass from 39 euros | www.sierraneva da.es)*. At weekends, when it can get very busy indeed, travelling by bus from Granada and booking your accommodation well in advance is highly recommended.

## SPAS & BATHS

Along the Costa del Sol a host of spas and hammams provide all manner of treatments. If you don't want to do without the sound of the sea, you can have a massage on a one of the Balinese beds on the beach at Puerto Banús. The interior of the ● *Hammam Al-Andalus (Plaza de los Mártires 5 | www.hammamalandalus.*

*com)* in Málaga is reminiscent of the Arab baths of the 14th century, with intricately fashioned arches and colourful Andalusian tiles. Relax on warm stones, have a massage or let your senses be captivated by sweet-smelling aromas.

## WIND & KITESURFING

The winds on the Andalusian Mediterranean coast are generally calm and ideal for windsurfing and kitesurfing beginners. On the Costa Tropical, *Windsurf La Herradura (Paseo Marítimo 34 | www.windsurf laherradura.com)* runs courses in La Herradura. On the Costa de Almería, *Sail & Surf (Playa Serena | tel. 6 59 04 77 92)* in Roquetas de Mar is a good place to try. For kiters, there's the *Freedom Kite School (Playa Guadalmansa and Ctra. de Cádiz km 164 | Hacienda Beach 86 | www.kite surfestepona.com)* in Estepona. *Kitesurf Málaga (www.kitesurfmalaga.com)* has no fixed base, but sets up at various spots along the western Costa del Sol. You will find stand-up paddle board rentals, like *Doble R. Paddle Surf (www.drpaddlesurf. com)* in Torremolinos, in all the large tourist centres.

The Costa del Sol and Costa Tropical are a little calmer than the surfer hotspot Tarifa on the Atlantic

# TRAVEL WITH KIDS

Late to bed, a school day starting at 9am, a 10-week summer holiday and never being told to be quiet – Spanish children have it really good. The country is considered child-friendly, with most people happy to see children out and about even late at night.

## ALMERÍA & COSTA DE ALMERÍA

**MARIO PARK** (133 D6) (*M5*)
Kamikaze slide, Río Bravo, Black Hole – these and other attractions guarantee summer water fun at this Aqua Park in Roquetas de Mar. *Open mid-June to beginning Sept daily 11am–7pm | 23.95 euros, children (height 0.90 m–1.40 m/3 ft–4 ft 5 in) 16.95 euros, from 3.30pm 17.95/ 12.95 euros | Camino de las Salinas | www. mariopark.com*

## OASYS – PARQUE TEMÁTICO DEL DESIERTO DE TABERNAS
(133 D5) (*M4*)
A duel, a gallows and stunts on horseback – the INSIDER TIP Wild West Show makes this Western film set, complete with saloon, bank and sheriff's office, really come alive. After all, this is where the likes of Clint Eastwood once trod the boardwalks. On top of that is the 'Desert Theme Park' with attractions ranging from a cactus garden, wagon museum and *cancan show (daily 1pm and 4pm, also at 7pm in summer)* to a cinema museum displaying film posters and ancient projectors. Most of the park is taken up

**Pony rides and petting zoos no longer quite cut it. How about the Wild West, crocodiles, circling birds of prey and dancing butterflies?**

by a zoo, with approx. 180 different species, including giraffes, rhinos and ostriches in a savannah habitat. There are parrot shows two or three times a day. The pool complex is open from June to mid-/end of Sept (included in admission fee; don't forget swimming gear). *July–beginning Sept daily 10am–9pm, Easter–June and rest of Sept/Oct 10am–6pm/7pm, Nov–Easter Sat/Sun 10am–6pm, approx. 15-min Western shows generally at noon and 5pm, in summer also at 8pm | 22.50 euros, children* *(aged 3–12) 12.50 euros, plus 2.90 euros parking fee | N 340 km 464 | www.oasys parquetematico.com*

### PARQUE DE LAS CIENCIAS
### GRANADA ● (131 E3) (*① J4*)

A tropical Butterfly House with butterflies *(mariposario tropical)* fluttering freely around, a replica of a dolmen, a planetarium, the 'Journey into the Human Body' pavilion: this educational but fun 'Science Park' will occupy children (and adults) for hours. The main focus is on interactive exhibits for kids. They can generate energy on a stationary bike, try out the INSIDER TIP *rolling ball sculpture 13* by Swiss artist Stefan Grünenfelder and literally get a feel for earth tremors on the earthquake simulator. Outside, there are regular falcon-

## PARQUE ORNITOLÓGICO LORO SEXI
**(131 E5) (*JJ J5*)**

Wild cries and shrieks will lead you to the Almuñécar Bird Park, on a sloping site adjacent to the lower ramparts of the castle. Some 200 species of birds, including parrots, cockatoos, peacocks and ibises, live here, many with gorgeous plumage, especially the Green and Hyacinth Macaws. The cactus garden is another point of in-

Siesta on the beach? But only with sunscreen!

ry displays *(rapaces en vuelo)*. The main landmark of the complex is the 🌿 *viewing tower (limited access, lunch break Tue–Sat)*; at a height of 37 m/121 ft, the platform offers panoramic views of the city and the highest summits of the Sierra Nevada; if you look through the free telescopes in winter, you'll even see skiers on the pistes. *Tue–Sat 10am–7pm, Sun 10am–3pm | incl. BioDomo 11 euros, under-18s 9 euros, Planetarium (programme usually only in Spanish) additional 2.50/2 euros | Av. de la Ciencia | www.parqueciencias.com*

terest on the site. *Oct–March Tue–Sun 10.30am–2pm and 4pm–6pm, April–June and Sept 10.30am–2pm and 5pm–8pm, July/Aug 10.30am–2pm and 6pm–9pm | 4 euros, children 2 euros | Calle Bikini 1, Plaza Abderramán | parquelorosexi. almunecar.es*

## COSTA DEL SOL AROUND MÁLAGA

**CROCODILE PARK** ● **(130 B6) (*JJ F6*)**
Over 250 giant reptiles, from crocodiles to alligators, live at the Crocodile Park

on the outskirts of Torremolinos. You can observe the beasts at close quarters in their open-air and indoor pools. The prize specimen is 'Big Daddy', all 1120 lbs of him. He is always in the midst of a small harem, and he once lost part of his tail in a fight with a rival. It's worth taking a look at one of the **INSIDER TIP** 'crocodile demonstrations' *(exhibiciones con cocodrilos | usually daily 11.30am, 1.30pm and 3.30pm, in summer also 5.30pm)* included in the admission fee. The tours (in English and Spanish) provide information on the characteristics and behaviour of the animals, which are sluggish on land but can strike in a split second in the water. The offspring of these primordial, cold-blooded creatures are kept at the breeding centre. *June–Sept daily 10am–7pm, March–May and Oct 10am–6pm, Nov–Feb 11am–5pm | 15.50 euros, children (aged 4–12) 13 euros | Calle Cuba 14 | www.cocodrilospark.com*

## COSTA DEL SOL AROUND MARBELLA

### INSIDER TIP MARIPOSARIO DE BENALMÁDENA (130 B6) (*M F6*)

A veritable riot of colour: green, turquoise, blue, orange. Around 1500 specimens from various tropical habitats in Africa, the Americas and Australia flutter around the butterfly house near the Buddha Temple in Benalmádena. Since butterflies usually only live for two to three weeks, there is a degree of fluctuation among the 150 species represented. The climatic conditions correspond to the their needs of the insects: a temperature of between 24 and 29 degrees Celcius and 80 per cent humidity. *Daily 10am–7.30pm | 10 euros, children (aged 3–12) 7.50 euros, reduced online rates | Calle Muérdago | Av. del Retamar | Benalmádena Pueblo | www.mariposariodebenalmadena.com*

### SELWO AVENTURA (130 E4) (*M E6*)

Half game enclosure and half zoo: 2000 animals live on this huge site. Travelling around on the 'safari trucks', kids will almost feel as though they're on a real safari. In the lakes area, Reserva de los Lagos, antelopes and gazelles leap around and elephants and giraffes have space in which to roam. There's lots of walking in Selwo Aventura, but it's not too far to the amazing bird canyon **INSIDER TIP** *Cañón de las Aves*. 340 m long and up to 25 m/82 ft high, the canyon, in which several hundred birds live among the bamboo and gum trees in relative freedom, is covered in netting. Towards the middle of the canyon, where the path leads uphill, look out for marabou storks. *Mid-Feb–Oct daily 10am–6pm (in summer until 7pm or 8pm), Nov–mid-Feb open only sporadically e. g. during the Christmas holidays | 24.50 euros, children (aged 3–10) 17 euros, reduced online rates from 15.90 euros | Las Lomas del Monte, signposted turn-off from the A7 at km 162.5*

The Crocodile Park is certainly no petting zoo

# FESTIVALS & EVENTS

Folklore and fireworks at saints' festivals, pulsating sounds at music festivals – in Andalusia there's always an excuse for a loud party. The only exception is the sombre mood during Holy Week (Semana Santa) processions, when in many places members of the numerous fraternities carry religious statues on gigantic floats, each of the hooded bearers taking a weight of around 54kg (120lbs).

## FESTIVALS & EVENTS

### JANUARY

2 Jan: The *Fiesta de la Toma* in Granada commemorates the capture of the city by the Christian troops in 1492.

5 Jan: In the evening are the *Three Wise Men Processions (Cabalgatas de los Reyes Magos)* with decorated floats, music groups and the distribution of sweets.

### MARCH/APRIL

During Holy week *(Semana Santa) Penitential Processions* take place in many places, often going on for hours. Granada and Málaga each have more than 30 fraternities and just as many processions taking place between Palm Sunday and Easter Sunday. They reach a climax on Maundy Thursday and Good Friday.

### MAY

3 May: *Cruces de Mayo* ('Festival of the Cross') is a spring festival with lots of floral decoration in the streets, in Granada and Almería.

### END MAY/BEGINNING JUNE

Major *Corpus Christi festival (Feria del Corpus)* in Granada

### JUNE

Around 11 June: *Feria de San Bernabé*, the festival of St Bernard, the patron saint of Marbella

### END JUNE–MID-JULY

Towards the end of June is the start of the *Festival de Música y Danza in Granada* (www.granadafestival.org), with ballet, INSIDER TIP flamenco performances and classical concerts.

### JULY

At the start of the month is the colourful *Feria* in Estepona, which lasts a week and incorporates a day fair and a night fair.

### JULY/AUGUST

INSIDER TIP *Starlite (www.starlitemarbella.com):* unique setting for this summer

festival in an open-air disco in a former quarry near Marbella. Music, fashion, art, cinema, food...

## AUGUST

On the first Saturday of the month, thousands head for the INSIDER TIP 'New Year Festival' (Fiesta de Nochevieja) in the Alpujarra village of Bérchules. The reason for the unusual date: a power cut in the middle of New Year celebrations in the mid-1990s. Ever since then, to be on the safe side, New Year has been celebrated in the summer.

15 Aug: In Cómpeta in the Nerja hinterland is the INSIDER TIP traditional wine festival of the *Noche del Vino*.

From around the middle of the month is the *Feria* in Málaga, accompanied by processions, concerts, flamenco, firework displays and bullfights. Other *local festivals* in the second half of August in Antequera and Almería; at the end of the month the *Feria* in Guadix begins with fireworks.

## SEPTEMBER

At the beginning of the month is the *Day of the Tourist* in Torremolinos, giant paella party and horse-drawn carriage display, *Pedro Romero festival* in Ronda and *Patron Saint's festival* in Mijas. *Flamenco festival* in the district of Albaicín in Granada.

## OCTOBER

Around 10 Oct: *Feria* in Fuengirola

## NATIONAL HOLIDAYS

If a holiday falls on a Sunday it is generally taken on the Monday.

| | |
|---|---|
| 1 Jan | Año Nuevo |
| 6 Jan | Reyes Magos |
| 28 Feb | Día de Andalucía |
| March/April | Maunday Thursday (Jueves Santo) |
| March/April | Good Friday (Viernes Santo) |
| 1 May | Día del Trabajo |
| 15 Aug | Asunción de Nuestra Señora |
| 12 Oct | Commemoration of the discovery of America (Día de la Hispanidad) |
| 1 Nov | Todos los Santos |
| 6 Dec | Constitution Day (Día de la Constitución) |
| 8 Dec | (Inmaculada Concepción) |
| 25 Dec | Navidad |

# LINKS, BLOGS, APPS & MORE

LINKS & BLOGS

www.visitcostadelsol.com Website for Málaga province and the Costa del Sol covering a broad range of topics, with plenty of information about the sights as well as cultural and leisure activities on the coast and in the hinterland

www.andalucia.com Well-established and very informative website covering a vast array of travel topics in the region, from flamenco classes to rural tourism, adventure sports to golf and festivals, and nightlife to flora & fauna

www.theolivepress.es Website with news and articles of local interest with an extensive section on eating out

andaluz.tv This site has news on Andalusia, with sections covering golf and the weather, and you can also click through the various webcams it has along the Costa del Sol

blog.andalucia.com Interesting range of subjects with constant new material. Linked to the andalucia.com website

www.malagaweb.com/blog Useful blog focused on forthcoming events

www.spainbymikerandolph.com A private blogger website by Mike Randolph. Short texts and striking, evocative photography make it well worth a click

www.couchsurfing.org Describes itself as the largest traveller community. You sign up with Facebook or email to find profiles of travellers or locals. Click 'Browse People' and then enter 'Marbella' or any number of Costa del Sol locations in the search field

www.expat-blog.com Click on "Destination", then "Spain" and select your area of interest. There is a large contingent of expatriate Brits on the Costa del Sol. This site has pictures, classified ads and a very lively forum. If you need specific information, then

Regardless of whether you are still preparing your trip or already on the Costa del Sol: these addresses will provide you with more information, videos and networks to make your holiday even more enjoyable

it's best to ask someone who lives there. It's also helpful if you're planning to relocate. There is another blog devoted to Málaga

www.whatgranada.com Online travel guide also featuring a series of videos covering many aspects of the city and the Alhambra. Besides information about the city proper, there are also links to other Spanish cities

Granada – Travel Guide minube Lots of tips on Granada created by the popular Spanish social network 'minube'

APPS

Beaching App Costa del Sol Nothing has been left out: pictures, descriptions and GPS coordinates for the beaches of Málaga province

SunTimer This app helps you calculate the length of time that you can lie in the sun without harm

WorldNomads, Rosetta Stone, L-Lingo and Duolingo  Look out for those brand names if you want to improve your Spanish using an app on your smart phone. Take your pick!

www.youtube.com/watch?v=xqxJMCQxb_Q The film is a good example of a solo classical flamenco performance

www.youtube.com/watch?v=LTu_npk4NFo Amore informal flamenco execution. Flamenco relies partly on traditional elements and partly on improvisation, so there is a lot of variety

www.360cities.net The 360° panoramic photos give an all-round view of top sights. Check out the views of the Alhambra, Málaga Cathedral, the Ronda bullfighting arena and many other attractions

360.visitacostadelsol.com/ENGLISH/webenglish/webenglish.html More stunning 360° images, this time from the Visit Costa del Sol website mentioned above

VIDEOS & MUSIC

# TRAVEL TIPS

## ACCOMMODATION

The choice ranges from the simple guesthouse (*pensión*; even more simple is a *fonda*) to the hostal (*hostal*) to hotels, which are classified on a scale of one to five stars. Good information on camping is provided by the website *www.vayacamping.net*. Country hotels and boutique hotels in the cities can be booked through the *Rusticae* chain (*www.rusticae.es*). You can find tips on rural accommodation (*turismo rural*) from *www.raar.es*; on villas in the Alpujarra region from *www.turismoalpujarra.com*, amongst others.

Prices for accommodation in Spain are mostly quoted without breakfast; hotels rarely include breakfast in the price of a room. In any case, it's often cheaper and better to go to a nearby bar of café. Beware: occasionally prices quoted for accommodation exclude value added tax

(IVA). If you book a double bed (*cama matrimonial*), you'll find yourself sleeping in a bed only 1.35 m/4.4 ft wide. If that's too narrow, choose twin beds (*camas separadas*).

## ARRIVAL

You should allow around two and a half to three days to get to Spain from the UK by car. The distance from London to Almería is 2300 km/1500 mi. The usual route is London–Paris–Marseille–Barcelona–València. Alternatively, take the ferry from Portsmouth to Bilbao/Santander and then drive down through Central Spain.

The journey by train can take up to 30 hours and include several changes of train. The cost will be much more than the cost of a flight booked well in advance. The state railway company, Renfe, offers foreign tourists the Renfe Spain Pass (*www.renfe.com/viajeros/viajes_internacionales/spainpass*), which is valid for all AVE high-speed trains on long- and medium-distance routes as well as for local trains into the centre and to the airport at Málaga. *www.renfe.com; www.seat61.com*

Buses belonging to Eurolines (*www.eurolines.co.uk*) regularly travel to Andalusia from various English cities, with destinations including Granada, Málaga and Almería. Depending on the place of departure and the destination the journey can take between 35–40 hours.

The region's international airports are in Málaga (large) and Alme-

## RESPONSIBLE TRAVEL

It doesn't take a lot to be environmentally friendly whilst travelling. Don't just think about your carbon footprint whilst flying to and from your holiday destination, but also about how you can protect nature and culture abroad. As a tourist it is especially important to respect nature, look out for local products, cycle instead of driving, save water and much more. If you would like to find out more about eco-tourism, please visit: *www.ecotourism.org*

ría (small). There are numerous flights all year round, but the airline schedules change all the time. The Spanish airlines are not generally renowned for their service, and frequent delays, unannounced cancellations and lost or damaged luggage have not helped their reputation. It's best to check schedules and prices directly with the airlines: *Ryanair (www.ryanair.com)* and *easyJet (www.easyjet.com)* depart from various British cities for Almería and Málaga. *Iberia (www.iberia.com)* and *British Airways (www.britishairways.com)* also fly to Almeria and Málaga.

## CAR HIRE

There's no shortage of places to hire a car, including at Málaga and Almería airports. However, hiring the car before you leave home is recommended; this not only guarantees availability but also costs much less. Weekly rates for a small model start at around 130 euros including unlimited mileage and fully comprehensive insurance, but the offers vary. Online agents such as *Auto Europe (www.auto-europe.co.uk)* enable you to compare prices easily.

It's always useful to watch out for financial pitfalls, such as the fuel policy *(política de gasolina):* when customers take charge of a car they have to pay an additional, previously unspecified, sum for a full tank, which, depending on the model, could be as much as 100 euros. You can return the car with an empty tank, but the sum you've already been charged will definitely be much more than the cost of filling the tank at a petrol station!

## CURRENCY CONVERTER

| £ | € | € | £ |
|---|---|---|---|
| 1 | 1.12 | 1 | 0.89 |
| 3 | 3.37 | 3 | 2.67 |
| 5 | 5.60 | 5 | 4.45 |
| 13 | 14.50 | 13 | 11.60 |
| 40 | 45 | 40 | 35.60 |
| 75 | 84 | 75 | 66.80 |
| 120 | 135 | 120 | 107 |
| 250 | 280 | 250 | 223 |
| 500 | 560 | 500 | 445 |

| $ | € | € | $ |
|---|---|---|---|
| 1 | 0.90 | 1 | 1.10 |
| 3 | 2.72 | 3 | 3.30 |
| 5 | 4.54 | 5 | 5.50 |
| 13 | 11.80 | 13 | 14.30 |
| 40 | 36.30 | 40 | 44 |
| 75 | 68 | 75 | 82.60 |
| 120 | 109 | 120 | 132 |
| 250 | 227 | 250 | 275 |
| 500 | 454 | 500 | 550 |

For current exchange rates see www.xe.com

## CLIMATE, WHEN TO GO

In high summer, the beaches of the Costa del Sol are often really packed. It's much more peaceful in the mild autumn and winter. Between January and April water temperatures in the Mediterranean have a maximum of 15°C (59°F).

Autumn and spring are perfect times of the year for walking and cycling, as well as taking a city break in Granada with extended excursions. That way you will escape the intense summer heat, which reaches 40°C (104°F) in some places, and avoid the queues and the traffic jams.

## CONSULATES & EMBASSIES

### UK CONSULATE
*Edificio Eurocom | Calle Mauricio Moro Pareto 2 | 29006 Málaga | tel. 9 52 3 23 00 | www.ukinspain.fco.gov.uk*

### US CONSULATE
*Edificio Lucio 1°-C | Avenida Juan Gómez Juanito 8 | 29640 Fuengirola | tel. 9 52 47 48 91 | es.usembassy.gov*

## CUSTOMS

Within the EU, items for personal use can be taken in and out of the country. Although there are no limits on the amount of alcohol and tobacco you can bring in from EU countries, the following guidelines apply: 800 cigarettes and 10 litres of spirits.

## DRIVING

The speed limits are: in urban areas 50 km/h (30 mph), on country roads – depending on the signing – 90 km/h (56 mph) and on motorways 120 km/h (75 mph), on certain stretches 130 km/h (80 mph). The drink-driving limit is 0.5 mg/g blood alcohol. Vehicles may not be towed away privately; this can only be done by authorised towing companies. Drivers must also keep a high-visibility jacket in the car as well as two warning triangles. There is a distinction between toll motorways *(autopista)* and similar but toll-free highways *(autovía)*. Spain has some of the worst accident rates in Europe. Nobody seems to pay much attention to pedestrian crossings. Keeping a safe distance from the car in front is a foreign concept and setting off on a red light is a habit that seems impossible to eradicate. If you're caught by the police for infringements such as using your mobile phone at the wheel, exceeding the speed limit or parking illegally, you'll have to pay a hefty fine. And it doesn't necessarily stop there; you may find your vehicle being towed away. Drivers who are not resident in Spain have to pay fines on the spot!

## ELECTRICITY

Mains voltage is 230 V. Remember to pack a universal adaptor.

## EMERGENCIES

There is one number for all emergencies: *112*. The police are called *policía*, the fire brigade *bomberos*, the ambulance service *ambulancia*.

## HEALTH

If you urgently need a doctor, ask for the closest hospital with an A and E depart-

# SPANISH ADDRESSES

Addresses in Spain are sometimes given without a number, in which case they are supplemented by *sin número,* shortened to 's/n'. The locals all know where each address is. If a house number is followed by another digit, this indicates the floor of the building; an additional letter can describe exactly where the apartment is on a particular floor: D stands for *derec* (right), I for *izquierda* (left) and C for *centro* (middle). A letter B *(for bajo)* means ground floor.

ment *(urgencia)*. The waiting times there can be very long.

If you have a European Health Insurance Card (EHIC), you will be treated free of charge by doctors, outpatient clinics and hospitals, which are part of the Spanish Seguridad Social system. If you go for treatment at a private practice or clinic, you have to pay on the spot and then submit the bill when you get home. It can therefore make sense to take out travel health insurance.

Chemists *(farmacias)* are everywhere and are well supplied. Some medication is available without prescription, and some drugs are cheaper than at home.

## IMMIGRATION

Identity card or passport is enough. If you're entering from a Schengen country there is usually no border control.

## INFORMATION

### SPANISH NATIONAL TOURISM OFFICES
Tourist information is available from the Spanish tourism offices and also at *www.spain.info*

– *6th Floor 64 North Row | London W1K 7DE | spaininfo@tourspain.es*
– *1395 Brickell Avenue, Suite 1130 | Miami, FL 33131 | miami@tourspain.es*
– *845 North Michigan Av, Suite 915-E | Chicago, IL 60611 | chicago@tourspain.es*
– *8383 Wilshire Blvd., Suite 960 | Beverly Hills, CA 90211 | losangeles@tourspain.es*
– *60 East 42nd Street, Suite 5300 (53rd Floor) | New York, NY 10165-0039 | oetny @tourspain.es*

Information in Spain is available from the respective local tourist information offices *(oficina de turismo)*; however, you can't rely 100 per cent on the accuracy of the material supplied, including addresses and opening times!

### TOURISM WEBSITES
*www.spain.info;*
*sierranevada.es;*
*www.turismoalmeria.org;*
*www.andalucia.org;*
*www.granadatur.com;*
*www.turgranada.es*

## BUDGETING

| | |
|---|---|
| Coffee | around 1.30 euros *for a café solo* |
| Petrol | around 1.40 euros *for 1 l of unleaded* |
| Bus travel | around 8–10 euros *for 100 km* |
| Lunch | from 9 euros *for a daily special* |
| Alhambra | 14 euros *admission charge* |
| Souvenirs | from 4 euros *for a small ceramic plate* |

## INTERNET ACCESS & WI-FI

Most hotels offer their guests free Wi-Fi, also known in Spanish as *wifi*. You will often also find public computer terminals in larger establishments. Bars and restaurants with internet hotspots are usually identified with black and white WIFI stickers. Those travelling without a smartphone, tablet or notebook should ask for a *locutorio*, where you can use a computer with an internet connection as well as make cheap calls abroad.

## MEDIA

There are more than 1000 different TV channels in Spain, including the main state-run channels TVE 1 and TVE 2 as well as the private Antena 3 and Tele 5. There are plenty of English-language channels as well, including BBC News 24 and CNN. English newspapers and magazines are available in the holiday resorts as well as in the larger towns, and, during the high season, the smaller ones. Regional newspapers such as 'Ideal' (Granada province) and 'Sur' (Málaga province) have useful information on events.

## MONEY & DISCOUNTS

Cash machines are widespread and major credit/debit cards such as Visa and MasterCard widely accepted in shops, restaurants and hotels. If paying by card, identification is occasionally required. Discounts on entry costs for museums and sights are generally available for children and frequently for students and pensioners. Some museums are free to enter once a week for the whole day or a couple of hours. Some *Andalusian museums* are free for EU citizens. *Málaga* (malagapass.com), *Granada* (granada tur.clorian.com) and *Almeria* (turismo dealmeria.org/en/travel-preparations/ almeria-card) all offer discount or tourist cards.

## NUDE SUNBATHING

Topless sunbathing on the beach is widespread; completely nude sunbathing is allowed only on explicitly designated beaches *(playas naturistas)* such as Cantarriján on the Costa Tropical as well as remote beaches such as exist in Cabo de Gata.

## OPENING HOURS

There are no fixed opening times for shops in Spain, but most are open Monday to Friday from 9.30am or 10am to 1.30pm or 2pm and from 4.30pm or 5pm to 8pm, Saturdays mornings only. In the holiday centres, many shops stay open right through the day and until late in the evening.

## PHONE & MOBILE PHONE

To call abroad, dial the prefix 00, then the country code (UK 0044, US 001), the area/city code without the 'zero' and the subscriber number. The code for Spain is 0034, afterwards you should dial the complete number. Within Spain no area code is necessary.

Mobile phones can be used without any difficulty; they always look for the network with the strongest frequency. If you want to phone a lot it's probably best to purchase a Spanish prepaid SIM card *(tarjeta prepagada)* so you can save on roaming fees. In Spain expensive 'service numbers' begin with 901 or 902; mobile numbers with 6 or 7.

## PHOTOGRAPHY

Memory cards and CDs tend to be more expensive in Spain, while branded batteries are often cheaper. Photography is forbidden in certain museums.

## POST

Postage for a standard letter up to 20 g or a postcard within Europe costs 1.40 euros at the time of printing. Stamps *(sellos)* are available from post offices and tobacconists *(estancos)* which you can recognise from the 'Tabacos' sign.

## PRICES

Even though income levels are lower than in the UK, the cost of living in Spain is about the same. Petrol, public transport and services are, however, cheaper than in the UK, as is a glass of wine and tapas in a bar.

Admission prices to sights and museums are between 2.50–4 euros, for famous destinations, such as the Picasso Museum in Málaga or the caves in Nerja, they are often twice or three times as much. Aquaparks and theme parks are generally very expensive.

## PUBLIC TRANSPORT

The bus network is excellent and the prices are relatively low. Every largish town has its own bus station (estación de autobuses). It's possible to travel the length of the Costa del Sol using commuter trains (trenes de cercanías) operated by the Spanish railway company Renfe (www.renfe.com), which run between Málaga and Fuengirola every 20–30 minutes. That way you will avoid the frequent traffic jams.

## TAXI

Hailing a taxi on the street is not very common – it is more usual to go to a taxi rank or call one up. Taxis are pretty cheap: minimum fare plus approx. 1–1.50 euros/km. Occasional additional surcharges.

## TIPPING

Satisfied customers at a restaurant generally leave a tip of around 5–10 per cent; in a taxi it is usual to round up the amount. Hotel staff will appreciate a tip of, say, 1 euro per day.

## WEATHER IN MÁLAGA

| | Jan | Feb | March | April | May | June | July | Aug | Sept | Oct | Nov | Dec |
|---|---|---|---|---|---|---|---|---|---|---|---|---|
| **Daytime temperatures in °C/°F** | 16/61 | 17/63 | 18/64 | 21/70 | 23/73 | 27/81 | 29/84 | 29/84 | 27/81 | 23/73 | 19/66 | 17/63 |
| **Nighttime temperatures in °C/°F** | 8/46 | 9/48 | 11/52 | 13/55 | 16/61 | 19/66 | 21/70 | 22/72 | 20/68 | 16/61 | 12/54 | 9/48 |
| ☀ Sunshine hours/day | 6 | 6 | 6 | 8 | 10 | 11 | 11 | 11 | 9 | 7 | 6 | 5 |
| ☂ Precipitation days/month | 5 | 5 | 6 | 3 | 2 | 1 | 0 | 0 | 2 | 4 | 6 | 5 |
| ≈ Water temperature in °C/°F | 15/59 | 14/57 | 14/57 | 15/59 | 17/63 | 18/64 | 21/70 | 22/72 | 21/70 | 19/66 | 17/63 | 16/61 |

☀ Sunshine hours/day  ☂ Precipitation days/month  ≈ Water temperature in °C/°F

# USEFUL PHRASES SPANISH

## PRONUNCIATION

| | |
|---|---|
| c | before 'e' and 'i' like 'th' in 'thin' |
| ch | as in English |
| g | before 'e' and 'i' like the 'ch' in Scottish 'loch' |
| gue, gui | like 'get', 'give' |
| que, qui | the 'u' is not spoken, i.e. 'ke', 'ki' |
| j | always like the 'ch' in Scottish 'loch' |
| ll | like 'lli' in 'million'; some speak it like 'y' in 'yet' |
| ñ | 'nj' |
| z | like 'th' in 'thin' |

### IN BRIEF

| | |
|---|---|
| Yes/No/Maybe | sí/no/quizás |
| Please/Thank you | por favor/gracias |
| Hello!/Goodbye!/See you | ¡Hola!/¡Adiós!/¡Hasta luego! |
| Good morning!/afternoon!/evening!/night! | ¡Buenos días!/¡Buenos días!/¡Buenas tardes!/¡Buenas noches! |
| Excuse me, please! | ¡Perdona!/¡Perdone! |
| May I ...?/Pardon? | ¿Puedo ...?/¿Cómo dice? |
| My name is ... | Me llamo ... |
| What's your name? | ¿Cómo se llama usted?/¿Cómo te llamas? |
| I'm from ... | Soy de ... |
| I would like to .../Have you got ...? | Querría .../¿Tiene usted ...? |
| How much is ...? | ¿Cuánto cuesta ...? |
| I (don't) like that | Esto (no) me gusta. |
| good/bad/broken/doesn't work | bien/mal/roto/no funciona |
| too much/much/little/all/nothing | demasiado/mucho/poco/todo/nada |
| Help!/Attention!/Caution! | ¡Socorro!/¡Atención!/¡Cuidado! |
| ambulance/police/fire brigade | ambulancia/policía/bomberos |
| May I take a photo here | ¿Podría fotografiar aquí? |

### DATE & TIME

| | |
|---|---|
| Monday/Tuesday/Wednesday | lunes/martes/miércoles |
| Thursday/Friday/Saturday | jueves/viernes/sábado |
| Sunday/working day/holiday | domingo/laborable/festivo |
| today/tomorrow/yesterday | hoy/mañana/ayer |
| hour/minute/second/moment | hora/minuto/segundo/momento |

# ¿Hablas español?

‚Do you speak Spanish?' This guide will help you to
say the basic words and phrases in Spanish.

| | |
|---|---|
| day/night/week/month/year | día/noche/semana/mes/año |
| now/immediately/before/after | ahora/enseguida/antes/después |
| What time is it? | ¿Qué hora es? |
| It's three o'clock/It's half past three | Son las tres/Son las tres y media |
| a quarter to four/a quarter past four | cuatro menos cuarto/ cuatro y cuarto |

## TRAVEL

| | |
|---|---|
| open/closed/opening times | abierto/cerrado/horario |
| entrance/exit | entrada/acceso salida |
| departure/arrival | salida/llegada |
| toilets/ladies/gentlemen | aseos/señoras/caballeros |
| free/occupied | libre/ocupado |
| (not) drinking water | agua (no) potable |
| Where is ...?/Where are ...? | ¿Dónde está ...? /¿Dónde están ...? |
| left/right | izquierda/derecha |
| straight ahead/back | recto/atrás |
| close/far | cerca/lejos |
| traffic lights/corner/crossing | semáforo/esquina/cruce |
| bus/tram/U-underground/taxi/cab | autobús/tranvía/metro/taxi |
| bus stop/cab stand | parada/parada de taxis |
| parking lot/parking garage | parking/garaje |
| street map/map | plano de la ciudad/mapa |
| train station/harbour/airport | estación/puerto/aeropuerto |
| ferry/quay | transbordador/muelle |
| schedule/ticket/supplement | horario/billete/suplemento |
| single/return | sencillo/ida y vuelta |
| train/track/platform | tren/vía/andén |
| delay/strike | retraso/huelga |
| I would like to rent ... | Querría ... alquilar |
| a car/a bicycle/a boat | un coche/una bicicleta/un barco |
| petrol/gas station/petrol/gas/diesel | gasolinera/gasolina/diesel |
| breakdown/repair shop | avería/taller |

## FOOD & DRINK

| | |
|---|---|
| Could you please book a table for tonight for four? | Resérvenos, por favor, una mesa para cuatro personas para hoy por la noche. |
| on the terrace/by the window | en la terraza/junto a la ventana |
| The menu, please | ¡El menú, por favor! |
| Could I please have ...? | ¿Podría traerme ... por favor? |
| bottle/carafe/glass | botella/jarra/vaso |

| | |
|---|---|
| knife/fork/spoon | cuchillo/tenedor/cuchara |
| salt/pepper/sugar | sal/pimienta/azúcar |
| vinegar/oil/milk/cream/lemon | vinagre/aceite/leche/limón |
| cold/too salty/not cooked | frío/demasiado salado/sin hacer |
| with/without ice/sparkling | con/sin hielo/gas |
| vegetarian/allergy | vegetariano/vegetariana/alergía |
| May I have the bill, please? | Querría pagar, por favor. |
| bill/receipt/tip | cuenta/recibo/propina |

## SHOPPING

| | |
|---|---|
| pharmacy/chemist | farmacia/droguería |
| baker/market | panadería/mercado |
| butcher/fishmonger | carnicería/pescadería |
| shopping centre/department store | centro comercial/grandes almacenes |
| shop/supermarket/kiosk | tienda/supermercado/quiosco |
| 100 grammes/1 kilo | cien gramos/un kilo |
| expensive/cheap/price/more/less | caro/barato/precio/más/menos |
| organically grown | de cultivo ecológico |

## ACCOMMODATION

| | |
|---|---|
| I have booked a room | He reservado una habitación. |
| Do you have any ... left? | ¿Tiene todavía..? |
| single room/double room | habitación individual/habitación doble |
| breakfast/half board/full board (American plan) | desayuno/media pensión/pensión completa |
| at the front/seafront/garden view | hacia delante/hacia el mar/hacia el jardín |
| shower/sit-down bath | ducha/baño |
| balcony/terrace | balcón/terraza |
| key/room card | llave/tarjeta |
| luggage/suitcase/bag | equipaje/maleta/bolso |
| swimming pool/spa/sauna | piscina/spa/sauna |
| soap/toilet paper/nappy (diaper) | jabón/papel higiénico/pañal |
| cot/high chair/nappy changing | cuna/trona/cambiar los pañales |
| deposit | anticipo/caución |

## BANKS, MONEY & CREDIT CARDS

| | |
|---|---|
| bank/ATM/pin code | banco/cajero automático/número secreto |
| cash/credit card | en efectivo/tarjeta de crédito |
| bill/coin/change | billete/moneda/cambio |

## HEALTH

| | |
|---|---|
| doctor/dentist/paediatrician | médico/dentista/pediatra |
| hospital/emergency clinic | hospital/urgencias |
| fever/pain/inflamed/injured | fiebre/dolor/inflamado/herido |
| diarrhoea/nausea/sunburn | diarrea/náusea/quemadura de sol |
| plaster/bandage/ointment/cream | tirita/vendaje/pomada/crema |
| pain reliever/tablet/suppository | calmante/comprimido/supositorio |

## POST, TELECOMMUNICATIONS & MEDIA

| | |
|---|---|
| stamp/letter/postcard | sello/carta/postal |
| I need a phone card/ | Necesito una tarjeta telefónica/ |
| I'm looking for a prepaid card for my mobile | Busco una tarjeta prepago para mi móvil |
| Where can I find internet access? | ¿Dónde encuentro un acceso a internet? |
| dial/connection/engaged | marcar/conexión/ocupado |
| socket/adapter/charger | enchufe/adaptador/cargador |
| computer/battery/rechargeable battery | ordenador/batería/batería recargable |
| e-mail address/at sign (@) | (dirección de) correo electrónico/arroba |
| internet address (URL) | dirección de internet |
| internet connection/wi-fi | conexión a internet/wifi |
| file/print | archivo/imprimir |

## LEISURE, SPORTS & BEACH

| | |
|---|---|
| beach/sunshade/lounger | playa/sombrilla/tumbona |
| low tide/high tide/current | marea baja/marea alta/corriente |
| cable car/chairlift | funicular/telesilla |

## NUMBERS

| | | | |
|---|---|---|---|
| 0 | cero | 14 | catorce |
| 1 | un, uno, una | 15 | quince |
| 2 | dos | 16 | dieciséis |
| 3 | tres | 17 | diecisiete |
| 4 | cuatro | 18 | dieciocho |
| 5 | cinco | 19 | diecinueve |
| 6 | seis | 20 | veinte |
| 7 | siete | 100 | cien, ciento |
| 8 | ocho | 200 | doscientos, doscientas |
| 9 | nueve | 1000 | mil |
| 10 | diez | 2000 | dos mil |
| 11 | once | 10 000 | diez mil |
| 12 | doce | 1/2 | medio |
| 13 | trece | 1/4 | un cuarto |

# ROAD ATLAS

The green line indicates the Discovery Tour 'Costa del Sol at a glance'
The blue line indicates the other Discovery Tours

**All tours are also marked on the pull-out map**

Photo: Beach near La Línea looking over to the Rock of Gibraltar